I0192025

As the pastor of a small, rural congregation that is walking the road of renewal, I can say this book speaks to the very heart of what God can do in a church <u>willing</u> to be revived. The principles shared here aren't just theory—they mirror the journey we've experienced firsthand: prayerful dependence, renewed vision, and a rediscovery of purpose in our community. This is more than a guide—it's a testimony of hope for every pastor, leader, and congregation longing to see new life where things once seemed stagnant. If God can breathe fresh life into our little church, He can do it anywhere. This book will help you believe that again.

Neal Smith, Pastor, Steadman Baptist Church
Leesville, South Carolina

For several years, NAMB has hosted an annual Replant Lab for associational leaders, and we've consistently encouraged attendees to take the training and make it their own. No one has taken that charge more to heart than Johnny Rumbough. Like the NAMB training, Johnny's renewal process is not theoretical or untested—it has been refined in real churches, with real leaders, over real time. I have pointed countless leaders to Johnny to learn from what he is doing, and I am genuinely excited that he has taken the time to put this process into a book. If you have met Johnny, you know he is a treasure to the churches he serves. I am confident this book will be a treasure to you and a gift to your ministry.

JimBo Stewart, Associate Director, Replant
North American Mission Board, SBC

Johnny Rumbough has been a friend and colleague for 20+ years. His book *"The Renewal Process: A Self-Led Practical Guide for Church and Associational Renewal"* is based on his personal experiences working with Lexington Baptist Association churches the past 29 years. *"The Renewal Process"* is a unique, process-oriented way to offer churches hope and direction that many have been missing. It is written in a clear, understandable, and easy-to-follow step-by-step process that helps them focus on rediscovering their first love. This process also offers associations, churches, and leaders a genuine sense of confidence, compassion, and credibility to self-lead. The book integrates both prayer and process, which provides power and progress for churches struggling, plateauing, or declining. It offers challenging questions, helpful insights, and real-life examples to help leaders self-lead from start to finish. Throughout this process, Johnny helps each congregation move toward a more mission-minded focus and a Spirit-led future. *"The Renewal Process"* is a great and practical resource for every association and pastor to have on hand.

Paul McKee, Director of Missions,
Association Mission Strategist,
Spartanburg County Baptist Network,
Spartanburg, South Carolina

THE RENEWAL PROCESS

A Self-Led Practical Guide for
Church and Association Renewal

JOHNNY RUMBOUGH

Copyright © 2026 by Johnny Rumbough
All rights reserved.
Printed in the United States of America

979-8-9933680-2-3

Scripture quotations are from the ESV® Bible (The Holy
Bible, English Standard Version®), copyright © 2001 by
Crossway, a publishing ministry of Good News Publishers.
Used by permission. All rights reserved.

Library of Congress Control Number: 2026902530

First Edition, 2026

Book Dedication

This book is dedicated to pastors, association mission strategists, and faithful leaders who have knelt in quiet rooms with tear-stained prayers, who have carried weighty burdens with trembling hands, and who have stood firm when the night felt long—confident that the God who raises dry bones still breathes life into His church, for the glory of His great name!

Contents

Foreword

If we are serious about reaching North America for Christ, we will be serious about church renewal. The North American Mission Board (NAMB), where I lead, is known for its emphasis on church planting, but we won't reach North America through new churches alone. We need the thousands and thousands of existing evangelical churches to be spiritually healthy, gospel lighthouses that are loving people and reaching their communities for Christ.

That is why NAMB has a team that focuses on working with churches that are on the verge of closing and helps them re-launch as a vibrant, outwardly focused congregation with a Great Commission focus.

It is also why I am so glad Johnny Rumbough has written this book. We need every good tool we can get our hands on that will help lead more churches back to health and back to an outward focus on their mission field.

The very first church I pastored, Hilltop Baptist Church in Fort Worth, Texas, was a reclamation project.

The congregation had dwindled down to seven members. While they voted me in seven to zero (my only unanimous call!), the difficult road to renewing that church came with challenges for both the church members and for me.

But as we waked through those challenges, we revitalized the church together. We sought the Lord together, witnessed to our community together, and over time saw those seven members grow to 50.

That growth didn't come because I was an expert in revitalization. This was my first time leading a church. I made some mistakes. At times I needed grace from the people I pastored and at other times I had to show grace to them.

There were lessons learned along the way. I still carry many of those lessons with me today as I serve in my current role.

In these pages, Johnny, who has worked alongside NAMB's Replant team, as well as hundreds of churches, has shared a host of practical tools that will help ministry leaders as they pursue renewal, whether in their churches or in associations.

Many of the experiences and lessons I've learned at my various ministry locations are represented in *The Renewal Process*. One of those, of course, is that there is not an easy, one-size-fits-all formula.

Some churches or associations need revitalizing in the aftermath of controversy or scandal, others simply because they lost focus of their mission as an organization or drifted into apathy. Those are radically different situations, and the road to health will not look the same.

Even though there's not a formula, we do serve a God who longs to see His people led into places of health and vitality, and as we follow His Spirit and study His Word, we will be able to identify some of the practical steps we can take to get to where He wants us to go.

Thousands of churches need to heed the call to pursue renewal so that, together, we may be ready to join the Lord in what He wants to do in our time.

What I love about Johnny's approach is its focus on leaning in to hear from the Lord, to focus on God's direction before building out a vision or strategy. As you reach, I hope you will pause, seek the Lord, and then follow the path He lays out for your church. I believe you'll witness His power and provision.

Dr. Kevin Ezell, President,
North American Mission Board, SBC

Preface

In the Fall of 2017, I attended a REPLANT LAB sponsored by the North American Mission Board of the Southern Baptist Convention. After attending this equipping conference, I felt equipped—with language, tools, and vision—to help struggling churches experience genuine renewal. Even as I was leading churches through the renewal process, I knew I wanted to write about the subject, so I began this book shortly thereafter.

"The Renewal Process" has led to many exciting experiences, conversations, speaking engagements, equipping opportunities, and coaching commitments, an astonishing outcome in light of the fact that it was birthed out of my own ministry need to help the local churches in my association. Improbable results like this are always difficult to explain, but conversations and experiences with peers who are also practitioners suggest that my learnings rang two bells loudly. First, struggling churches are tired and ready to experience a better future and say, *Yes!* Second, leaders found the six-stage renewal process framework, presented visually as a funnel graph, practical and effective. It made sense as a roadmap and helped people talk about transformation, renewal needs, and the solution presented through the renewal process.

Part 1: The Renewal Challenge and Its Solution

I've tried to build on both of these virtues in writing this book, and to add a few more. It is hands-on and practical. I've also been more explicit in linking the discussion back to the engine that drives the solution process—and in showing how a purely program mindset inevitably fails, regardless of the quality of the leaders involved.

Those familiar with my church and associational renewal experiences know that they integrate and extend the six-stage renewal process originally developed by NAMB's Replant LAB. This book is a logical extension of NAMB's equipping and my past experiences of leading churches and associations in their journey of renewal.

A number of people have influenced the content in this book. They include Henry and Richard Blackaby's *Spiritual Leadership*—A powerful reminder that true transformation flows from intimacy with God. Their call to lead from the overflow of a surrendered heart has deeply shaped the spiritual foundation of this renewal process; Tom Cheyney's *Revitalize Network: Renewing Church and Leaders*—His passionate leadership in church revitalization has inspired countless pastors and associational leaders to believe again in the transforming power of the Gospel to bring new life to declining churches; Mark Clifton's *Reclaiming Glory: Revitalizing Dying Church*—His clear voice on church replanting has deeply shaped the way many of us think about dying churches and resurrection hope; Mark Hallock's *Replant Road*—A clear practical guide for leading struggling churches toward renewed health. His emphasis on prayerful dependence, patient leadership, and gospel-centered restoration has deeply influenced my understanding of how renewal takes place in churches and associations; John Kotter's *Leading Change*—His insights on establishing urgency, building momentum, and embedding change into culture helped shape how I understand and communicate the process of lasting renewal within churches and associations; and Thom Rainer's *Anatomy of a Revitalized Church*—A clear and compassionate look into the principles that lead declining churches toward renewed vitality.

These voices, along with countless unnamed mentors, missionaries, professors, and faithful church members, have influenced my thinking and stirred my soul. I offer this work in the same spirit of humility and hope—that the Church might live again, fully awake, fully alive, and fully centered on the Gospel of Jesus Christ.

At its core, the Renewal Process is simply a pathway for God's people to hear His voice again, to return to their first love, and to align with His mission in their generation.

Every generation needs its own Pentecost—not a repeat of history, but a fresh wind of the same Spirit. What began in the Upper Room still continues today, in sanctuaries and fellowship halls, in leadership teams and prayer groups, in every humble heart that says, *"Come, Holy Spirit."*

"The Lord your God is in your midst...He will rejoice over you with gladness; He will quiet you by His love; He will exult over you with loud singing."—Zephaniah 3:17

PART I

The Renewal Challenge

and

Its Solution

CHAPTER 1

Why Process Works and Programs Fail

"Christ loved the church and gave Himself up for her."
—Ephesians 5:25

Dying churches do not bring God glory. Declining church attendance and a significant number of church closures are the fruit of the need for church and associational renewal.

The real need for church renewal arises from both spiritual and practical realities that affect the health and mission of the local church.

Many churches drift from their first love, Christ (Revelation 2:4). Over time, routine replaces passion, and maintenance replaces mission. Church renewal calls God's people back to spiritual vitality, restoring their dependence on the Holy Spirit, prayer, and the centrality of the Gospel. It's about rekindling a relationship with God.

Part 1: The Renewal Challenge and Its Solution

In the latest *Pew Research Center Religious Landscape Study* (2023-34), 62% of Americans identify as Christian—down from 78% in 2007. Concerning church attendance, according to the same Pew study, only 33% of U.S. adults say they attend religious services in person once a month.[1]

According to a *Gallup* article published on March 25, 2024, reporting on all religions, "Three in ten Americans say they attend religious services every week (21%) or almost every week (9%)."[2] In the same article, Gallup states, "Two decades ago, an average of 42% of U.S. adults attended religious services every week or nearly every week."

In my own denomination, the Southern Baptist Convention, we are experiencing an average of 800 church closures a year, according to Mark Clifton (senior director of replanting for the North American Mission Board, SBC), speaking at a 2023 event. Clifton noted that approximately 90% of the church closures in the SBC are in neighborhoods that experienced growth in the previous decade.[3]

My Story of The Renewal Process

Every meaningful idea is born from a burden. The Renewal Process was born from many.

For decades, I've walked with churches and associations that have lost their sense of direction. Some were declining, others plateaued, and a few were holding steady but quietly wondering, *"Is this all God has for us?"* Across countless conversations, I saw the same eyes of frustration—the look of leaders who loved their people deeply yet couldn't find a clear path forward.

That longing—to help God's people move from confusion to clarity—became the seed of something greater.

It was during a conference titled *The Replant LAB*, conducted by the North American Mission Board of the Southern Baptist Convention, that I was first introduced to and trained in the six stages of the renewal process.

Renewal Is Not a Program

Most churches and associations do not lack activity. They lack clarity.

Calendars are full. Committees still meet. Worship still happens. Ministries still operate. Yet beneath the motion, there is often a quiet, shared awareness among leaders: *something is no longer aligned.* The fruit does not match the effort. The energy does not reflect the vision. The structures that once served the mission now strain to sustain it.

When this tension grows, leaders naturally begin to search for answers. They look for resources, strategies, consultants, or programs that promise renewal—often defined as growth, revitalization, or momentum regained. The hope is understandable. But it is here, at the very beginning, that an important distinction must be made.

Renewal is not a program. Programs can be adopted quickly. Renewal cannot. Programs promise outcomes. Renewal requires discernment. Programs focus on implementation. Renewal begins with truth.

This guide does not offer a shortcut, a silver bullet, or a guaranteed result. It offers something slower, harder, and ultimately more faithful: a process designed to help churches and associations tell the *truth, listen carefully*, and *discern wisely* what obedience looks like in their unique context.

Renewal Begins with Returning, Not Reinventing

Biblically, renewal is not innovation for its own sake. It is not trend-chasing, rebranding, or restructuring driven by anxiety. Renewal is a return—a reorientation of heart, mission, and practice toward faithfulness.

Throughout Scripture, renewal follows a pattern: God's people pause, listen, repent, remember, and respond. Renewal exposes before it restores. It clarifies before it mobilizes. And often, it disrupts before it heals.

This is why renewal cannot be rushed.

Many leaders feel pressure to do *something*—to act decisively, implement change quickly, or prove progress visibly. But speed without discernment often leads to deeper confusion. Momentum without alignment only accelerates decline.

The Renewal Process is intentionally designed to slow leaders down—not to stall obedience, but to protect it. It creates space for prayer, listening, honest assessment, and shared understanding before decisions are made.

Why Churches and Associations Need a Process

Churches and associations don't fail because they lack faith. They falter because they lack focus.

Over time, ministries accumulate layers—programs that once served a purpose but now drain energy, traditions that once brought unity but now divide. Without realizing it, leaders wake up surrounded by activity but devoid of direction. They're doing many things, but few that move the mission forward.

The Renewal Process helps leaders rediscover their direction. It shows that renewal isn't an instant miracle or a random burst of energy—it's the result of a Spirit-led journey through stages of listening, clarifying, uniting, and acting **that leads to a future that brings God great glory!**

The Renewal Process provides language for that journey. It helps a pastor or an associational leader know where they are and say, *"We're not stuck; we're in Stage 2,"* or, *"We're not failing; we're examining."* That alone can bring tremendous peace, unity, confidence, and awareness. When you can name where you are, you can begin to move toward what's next, **toward a future that brings God great glory!**

Why Programs Often Fail

Programs are attractive because they offer clarity without cost. They define steps, promise timelines, and imply results. They assume readiness. They reward activity. And they often bypass the harder work of alignment, trust-building, and grief.

Renewal processes, on the other hand, do not promise outcomes. They reveal realities.

A faithful process may confirm the current direction—or it may uncover misalignment. It may lead to revitalization—or it may lead to replanting, restructuring, or even a faithful conclusion of ministry as it has been known. None of these outcomes is a failure. Each can be an expression of obedience.

This is why many churches resist true renewal. Renewal asks questions before offering answers. It requires humility before strategy. It insists that leaders listen not only to data and voices, but to the Spirit of God.

Programs ask, *What should we do next?* Renewal asks, *Who are we called to be—and what is God inviting us to release or embrace?*

Seeing the Renewal Process as Movement

The Renewal Process illustrated through the Funnel Graph *(featured on this book's front cover)* is more than a diagram—it's a picture of movement. Every organization that is alive is in a state of motion. The question is whether that motion is purposely directed or unintentionally drifting.

When leaders lose a sense of direction, they often double their activity instead of clarifying their purpose. The Renewal Process, illustrated using the Funnel Graph, clearly identifies the direction.

To the left of the funnel is the **Exploration Stage**—the wide, spacious season where we pray, ask questions, and seek understanding. We gather stories and data, listen to our people, and invite the Holy Spirit to speak.

Then comes the **Examination Stage**—honest evaluation of where we are. It's not about blame; its about truth. What's working? What's not? Where have we drifted from our mission?

Next comes the **Presentation Stage**—sharing discoveries with others. It's the moment of communication and invitation, when leaders begin to bring others into the conversation.

The **Recommendation Stage**—turning insight into direction. Leaders begin shaping practical steps, always asking, *"What is God calling us to do next?"*

After that is the **Affirmation Stage**—a critical stage where the body of believers unites around what's been discerned. Decisions are made prayerfully, with ownership and unity.

Finally comes the **Implementation Stage**—where the plan becomes practice, and the Spirit breathes fresh life into the people of God.

Each stage narrows the focus, moving from the broad work of discovery to the specific work of obedience. The further you go, the clearer and more aligned the mission becomes.

Why the Renewal Process Works

I've often said that God is not just the God of miracles— He's also the God of process. That's why The Renewal Process works: it honors God the way God works.

Starting at the wide end, the process is highly relational and prayerful. As it moves toward the narrow end, it becomes more structured and actionable. Spirit and structure meet at every stage—neither competing nor contradicting, but complementing one another.

Too often, churches and associations either over-spiritualize (*"Let's just pray and wait"*) or over-systematize (*"Let's just plan and act"*). The Renewal Process calls for both prayer *and* process. Without prayer, the plan lacks power. Without process, the prayer lacks progress.

Who This Guide Is For—and Who It Is Not

This guide is written for churches and associations willing to engage honestly with their current reality. It is for pastors, AMSs, elders, deacons, staff, and leadership teams who are open to discernment, even when the outcome is unclear.

This guide is **not** for churches seeking a quick fix. It is not for leaders looking to validate predetermined decisions. It is not for groups unwilling to listen to dissenting voices or confront uncomfortable truths.

The Renewal Process assumes courage, patience, and prayer. It invites leaders into a shared journey—not a guaranteed destination, but toward greater clarity and trust.

The Role of the Leader

Every renewal process needs a guide—**a leader who understands both the patience of the process and the urgency of the mission**. Leading renewal isn't about pushing people through stages. It's about walking with them through the process of discernment.

When I facilitate the Renewal Process in churches and associations, I remind the leaders that the journey is rarely smooth. There will be tension, fatigue, and resistance. But when leaders stay calm, prayerful, and consistent, the process itself becomes a discipling experience.

It's not only the larger body of the church or association that is renewed—the leaders themselves experience renewal.

One association mission strategist told me, *"This process didn't just change our churches; it changed me. It made me slow down and listen again to God, to His people, and to my own calling."*

That's the beauty of the Renewal Process: it forms the soul of the leaders as much as it shapes the future of the church and association.

Prayerfully, you will find the guidance and tools needed to self-lead your church or association through renewal, within these pages.

A Gentle but Necessary Warning

Engaging in renewal always carries risk. The risk is not failure—it is honesty.

As truth surfaces, long-held assumptions may be challenged. Sacred cows may be questioned. Grief may emerge—for what once was, for what was lost, or for what never became.

Renewal often reveals that not everything can be carried forward. This process may lead to change. It may lead to redirection. It may lead to release. Each of these can be faithful responses when discerned prayerfully and embraced together. What matters most is not the outcome, but the posture with which the journey is undertaken.

Preparing to Begin

Before moving further, it is important to pause. Renewal does not begin with Stage One. It begins with readiness—with leaders willing to slow down, listen well, and commit to walking together honestly.

The chapters that follow will lay the foundation for that journey. They will explain the framework, clarify the process, and prepare you for the work ahead. The stages themselves will come soon enough.

For now, the invitation is simple:
Be patient.
Be prayerful.
Be willing to tell the truth.
Renewal is not a program. It is a process of discernment—
and it begins here.

A Biblical Reflection

In Ezekiel 37, God showed the prophet a valley full of dry
bones. The Lord asked the question that still echoes in the
hallways and auditoriums of churches today: *"Can these
bones live?"*

Ezekiel wisely answered, *"Lord, you know."*

So, it was then that God began a process:
    First, the bones came together—structure.
    Then, flesh formed—organization.
    Finally, breath entered—Spirit.

It was both orderly and miraculous. The same is true for
renewal in churches (and associations) today.
    The bones must come together (structure).
    The flesh must form (organization).
    Then the breath must come (Spirit).

Without structure, there is chaos. Without the Spirit, there is death. The Renewal Process understands the importance of both.

I believe Ezekiel 37 is a reminder that renewal for the church (and the same is true for the association) isn't always an instant resurrection—it's often a divinely guided, Spirit-led process. It is bones coming together and breath filling them again.

A Word of Encouragement

As you're reading this book, you probably sense a stirring—a quiet conviction that your church, association, or network of churches could be experiencing more Kingdom impact than it is today.

Maybe you've tried before and feel weary.

Maybe you've been faithful for years, but are hungry for fresh direction.

Maybe you've simply lost sight of what's next.

Wherever you are, the good news is this: renewal is possible. God is not finished with His church, and He's not finished with you.

The Renewal Process is not a formula—it's a framework. It doesn't promise ease, but it offers clarity. It helps leaders slow down, listen, discern, and move with confidence.

I've seen declining congregations find purpose again.
I've seen associations rediscover unity after years of
tension.
I've seen pastors regain joy in ministry.

In every case, the Renewal Process was simply a tool God
used to breathe life into dry bones. And He can do the same
for you and your church or association.

Reflection Questions

1. Where are you right now? Are you exploring, examining,
presenting, recommending, affirming, or implementing?

2. Is your church or association struggling? What would it
look like for breath to return?

3. What is God saying? Exploration always begins with
spiritual discernment, not strategic urgency.

4. Who's walking with you? Renewal rarely happens alone.

Closing Thought

In every generation, God raises up leaders who dare to
believe that dead bones can live again. They don't begin with
strategy; they begin with surrender.

CHAPTER 2

Successful Renewal and the Process That Leads It

"And I am sure of this, that he who began a good work in you will bring to completion at the day of Jesus Christ."
—Philippians 1:6

In ministry, we often celebrate moments and overlook *movements*. We rejoice when someone is baptized, when a new family joins, or when a breakthrough happens in prayer. But beneath every visible fruit, there's usually been a long, unseen process—small decisions, quiet prayers, patient waiting, faithful obedience.

The Renewal Process is built on this truth: **God works through process.** He could do everything instantly, but He chooses to shape people through time, tension, and transformation. The same is true for churches and associations. Renewal rarely happens in a flash of inspiration. It's born through the slow, steady rhythm of listening, clarifying, aligning, and obeying.

Part 1: The Renewal Challenge and Its Solutions

The Renewal Process is intentionally designed to move from **wide listening** to **focused discernment**. The Funnel Graph (*featured on this book's front cover*) visually represents this journey. It is not a strategy for efficiency, nor a mechanism for control. It is a safeguard—protecting leaders from premature decision-making while guiding them toward faithful clarity.

Before engaging the stages of the process, it is important to understand what the Funnel Graph is—and what it is not.

What the Funnel Graph Is

In seasons of uncertainty, churches and associations often experience one of two extremes. Some remain stuck in endless discussion, unable to move forward with confidence. Others rush to solutions, mistaking speed for decisiveness. Both responses are understandable—and both can be harmful.

The Funnel Graph offers a different path.

On the left side of the funnel, the space is wide and open. Voices are many. Questions are open. Listening is prioritized over conclusions. As the process unfolds, the funnel narrows toward the right—not to exclude voices, but to increase clarity. Each stage reduces ambiguity, aligns understanding, and builds shared ownership. By the time decisions are made, they are not sudden. They are the natural result of a faithful process.

What the Funnel Graph Is Not

Before describing how the Funnel Graph works, it is important to clarify several misconceptions.

The Funnel Graph is **not**:
- A tool for manipulating outcomes.
- A way to justify decisions already made.
- A shortcut to change.
- A consultant-driven model that removes local leadership responsibility.

Instead, it is a **self-led framework for discernment**. It belongs to the church or association engaging it. Outside help may support the process, but ownership always remains local.

The funnel does not dictate what the outcome must be. It clarifies *how* the outcome is discerned.

God's Way Has Always Been a Process

From the very first page of Scripture, we see that God is not random—He is orderly. Creation itself unfolds day by day, stage by stage. He didn't speak everything into existence at once. Instead, He separated light from darkness, sky from land, and sea from shore. He built the world in a rhythm that revealed His wisdom.

When He delivered Israel from Egypt, He didn't transport them instantly to the Promised Land. He led them step by step through the wilderness and the waiting. Why? Because the journey wasn't just about getting them to a place—it was about forming them into a people.

Even Jesus embraced process. He began His public ministry with a season of preparation, called disciples one at a time, and spent three years developing them before sending them out. After His resurrection, He instructed them to wait for the Holy Spirit before beginning their mission. God's plan unfolds through process because process transforms us.

That's why *process-thinking* is not just practical leadership—it's spiritual obedience. When leaders resist process, they often resist the very way God works.

The Movement: Exploration to Implementation

The Funnel Graph is built around six distinct stages. Each stage has a purpose, a posture, and a set of guiding questions. Together, they form a coherent journey from listening to action.

The movement is intentional:

- **Exploration** opens the conversation. Opens hearts to listen to God and one another.
- **Examination** assesses reality. Opens eyes to the truth about the present.
- **Presentation** tells the truth clearly. Opens dialogue that builds understanding.
- **Recommendation** narrows possible pathways. Opens direction and shared possibilities.
- **Affirmation** builds shared ownership. Opens unity and commitment.
- **Implementation** puts discerned decisions into practice. Opens action and culture change.

Each stage narrows the funnel slightly—not by pressure, but by clarity. Notice the pattern: each stage opens something new. The Renewal Process isn't about closing doors—it's about opening the right ones in the right order.

Leaders often want to skip ahead, especially when answers seem obvious. The funnel resists that temptation. It insists that understanding precedes agreement, and that agreement precedes action.

By the end, what was once scattered becomes aligned. What was confusing becomes clear. And what was dying begins to live.

Why Narrowing Builds Trust

Narrowing can feel threatening. Leaders may fear that as the funnel tightens, voices will be silenced or decisions forced. In reality, the opposite is true when the process is honored.

The widest listening happens early. The deepest understanding forms in the middle. The strongest alignment emerges near the end.

Because leaders and members have been heard, informed, and engaged along the way, trust grows rather than diminishes. Decisions feel owned, not imposed.

This is why the Funnel Graph protects unity. It does not eliminate disagreement, but it creates a shared journey that reduces surprise and suspicion.

How the Funnel Graph Shapes Thinking

When you adopt a *process* mindset, you begin to see patterns. Instead of reacting to every crisis, you start asking,

"Where are we in this process?" and *"What is God doing here?"*

That shift alone changes everything. It keeps you calm in confusion and patient in progress.

Let's look at how process-thinking transforms the leader's perspective:

- **From Events to Journeys:**
  You stop seeing success as one-time wins and start seeing it as an ongoing movement.

- **From Panic to Peace:**
  When you know where you are in the process, you stop overreacting to delays or resistance. You recognize them as normal parts of development.

- **From Control to Cooperation:**
  Process-thinking moves leadership from *"How can I make this happen?"* to *"How can I join what God is doing?"*

This is how healthy renewal unfolds—through leaders who think long-term, pray consistently, and trust the process even when results are still unseen.

The Role of Leadership Within the Funnel

Leadership posture shifts as the funnel narrows. Early in the process, leaders are **listeners and facilitators**. They create space for voices, questions, and prayer. Later, leaders become **interpreters and guides**, helping the church or association make sense of what has been heard. Near the end, leaders step into **shepherding and stewardship**, calling the body to respond faithfully to what has been discerned.

At no point are leaders passive. But their role evolves—from opening space, to framing truth, to guiding action.

The Funnel Graph provides leaders with permission to lead differently at different times.

Guardrails That Protect the Process

The Funnel Graph includes built-in guardrails designed to prevent common failures:

- **No stage is rushed.** Movement happens only when clarity is sufficient.
- **No stage is skipped.** Each contributes something essential.
- **No decision is final before Affirmation.** Ownership matters.
- **No implementation occurs without alignment.** Action follows agreement.

These guardrails may feel slow, especially to leaders accustomed to decisive action. But they prevent far greater delays caused by resistance, confusion, or division later.

The Role of Patience in the Renewal Process

Patience is not passive waiting—it's active trust. It's what allows leaders to keep sowing when they don't yet see fruit.

When Paul wrote, *"Let us not grow weary in doing good, for the proper time we will reap a harvest if we do not give up"* (Galatians 6:9), he was describing process-thinking. The harvest comes not to the hurried but to the steadfast.

Patience keeps us from mistaking progress for failure. It gives us eyes to see God's invisible work while we walk faithfully through The Renewal Process.

Process Protects Against Burnout

One of the hidden gifts of process thinking is that it guards leaders from burnout.

When you operate without a process, every problem feels personal. Every setback feels final.

However, when you understand the Renewal Process using the Funnel Graph, you realize that each obstacle is a part of the journey. You stop measuring success by this week's attendance or next month's giving, and start measuring it by faithfulness to the stage you're in.

That doesn't mean you ignore results—it means you interpret them through a *process* lens. You learn to say, *"We're in the examination stage right now; it's okay that things feel unsettled."* That perspective frees churches (or associations) to breathe again.

How Process Thinking Builds Health

Healthy churches or associations don't chase fads: they build foundations. They understand process-thinking.

Process thinking builds long-term health by cultivating three things:

1. **Clarity.**

People know where they are and where they're going. Confusion decreases, communication improves.

2. **Alignment.**

Ministries and decisions start pulling in the same direction. Energy is not wasted on competing priorities.

3. **Momentum.**

Because clarity and alignment exist, progress feels natural rather than forced. People begin to anticipate the next step rather than resist it.

Health doesn't come from speed—it comes from steady, Spirit-guided process.

Who Leads the Process

The Renewal Process is primarily the work of a **smaller leadership group**—often a designated Renewal Team, leadership council, or executive team. *(Note: This group is typically formed at the outset of the church or association's* *decision to engage in the Renewal Process formally. It usually consists of seven members.)* While broader voices inform the process, this renewal process requires concentrated discernment.

This does not diminish the importance of participation. It honors it by ensuring that information gathered and recommendations presented are formed carefully, prayerfully, and responsibly.

The renewal team should be:
- Trusted.
- Representative.
- Prayerful.
- Willing to hold tension.

The credibility of the Renewal Process depends on the integrity of those entrusted with it.

A Leader's Prayer

Lord, teach me the power of Your process.
Help me trust that every stage has purpose.
Guard me from impatience and pride.
When I can't see results, remind me that
You're still at work.
Shape my leadership not by what I can control, but by how
faithfully I can cooperate with You.

Part 1: The Renewal Challenge and Its Solutions

Make me a shepherd who honors Your timing, and a leader who never stops believing that renewal is worth the wait.

Reflective Questions

1. How have you seen God use process to shape you personally or your ministry?

2. Which stage of The Renewal Process are you most tempted to rush through? Why?

3. What might change in your leadership if you viewed delays as divine design instead of failure?

4. Who around you needs encouragement to trust the process rather than escape it?

Closing Thought

The power of process is not in its structure—it's in its surrender. When leaders slow down enough to listen, when they honor each stage, when they allow God to work in His rhythm rather than theirs, the results are deeper than numbers—they're eternal.

Moments inspire. Processes transform. And, when God's people commit to His process, the bones begin to live again.

PART II

The Six-Stage Renewal Process

The CORE of the Book

(Chapters 3-8)

Part II: The Six-Stage Process

CHAPTER THREE

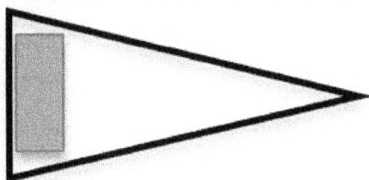

Stage 1

Exploration
What is God saying?

"You will seek me and find me, when you seek me with all of your heart."—Jeremiah 29:13

The Renewal Process begins the journey of discovery with the question, ***"What is God saying?"***

That single question has the power to reorient an entire church or association. Before plans are drawn, before committees are formed, before goals are set—renewal leaders must pause and listen to what God is saying.

Welcome to the **Exploration Stage**, where the renewal process begins.

Exploration is the wide end of the funnel, as described in previous chapters and illustrated by the Funnel Graph example. It's the season of holy curiosity—where we pray, watch, and discern what the Spirit of God is revealing. Without this stage, the rest of the funnel becomes little more than human effort wrapped in religious language.

Every genuine movement of spiritual renewal begins when leaders stop talking long enough to listen to what God is saying.

Exploration is the discipline of listening before labeling. It is the widest side of the funnel and the most easily misunderstood stage of the Renewal Process. Leaders often feel pressure to move quickly toward answers, especially when concerns are already known or assumptions feel obvious. Exploration resists that pressure. It creates space— not for speculation, but for prayerful attentiveness.

This stage does not ask, *What should we do?*
It asks, *What is happening—and how is God inviting us to listen?*

The Purpose of the Exploration Stage

The primary purpose of Exploration is **understanding**, not evaluation. It is about gathering perspectives, stories, and observations without attempting to fix or explain them.

Exploration allows leaders to hear:
- How people experience the church or association.
- What concerns are being carried quietly.
- Where hope still exists.
- What questions are surfacing across generations and roles.

At this stage, clarity comes through **breadth**, not depth. The goal is not consensus. It is awareness.

The Posture Required for Exploration

Exploration requires a specific leadership posture—one that may feel counterintuitive.

Leaders must:
- Listen without correcting.
- Receive feedback without defending.
- Resist explaining intentions.
- Avoid evaluating comments in real time.

This posture communicates safety. It reassures participants that the purpose is not to judge or persuade, but to understand. Without this posture, Exploration quickly collapses into debate or justification. Leaders should remember: **listening is not agreement**. It is respect.

Who Should Be Involved In Exploration

Because Exploration is the widest part of the funnel, participation should be broad and inclusive.

This may include:
- Key leaders and staff.
- Long-term members.
- Newer participants.
- Ministry volunteers.
- Community partners.

Exploration honors the belief that understanding emerges best when leaders listen beyond their own circles.

What Exploration Is—and Is Not

Clarity at this stage depends on discipline.

Exploration IS:
- Listening without an agenda.
- Asking open-ended questions.
- Collecting perspectives.
- Praying for insight.

Exploration IS NOT:
- A problem-solving session.
- A town hall for debate.

- A survey designed to confirm assumptions.
- A platform for persuasion.

When Exploration is rushed or repurposed, it loses its integrity—and the funnel narrows too soon.

Guiding Questions for Exploration

Rather than structured assessments, Exploration relies on **open, invitational questions**. These questions invite storytelling rather than opinions.

Examples include:
- *What do you value most about this church or association?*
- *Where do you sense energy or hope right now?*
- *What concerns you about our future?*
- *What do you believe God may be inviting us to notice?*

Leaders should listen for themes, not solutions. Repetition matters more than passion. Silence matters as much as speech.

Common Pitfalls in Exploration

Even well-intentioned leaders can unintentionally derail this stage. Common pitfalls include:
- Moving too quickly to interpretation.

- Allowing dominant voices to shape the conversation.
- Using language that implies judgment.
- Responding defensively to hard truths.
- Treating Exploration as a formality.

When these occur, trust erodes. Leaders may need to slow down, restate the purpose, or even pause the process to reset posture.

Biblical Foundation for Exploration

Throughout Scripture, every great movement of God begins with exploration—a season of seeking before doing.

- **Moses** didn't march into Egypt until he first heard God from the burning bush.
- **Nehemiah** walked through Jerusalem at night, exploring the ruins before making a plan.
- **Jesus** spent forty days in the wilderness before launching His public ministry.
- **The apostles** prayed and waited for the Holy Spirit before taking the Gospel to the nations.

Exploration precedes mission because revelation precedes direction. God's people move only after *hearing* from God.

Why Some May Skip This Stage

Most leaders love action. We're wired to fix, to plan, to

move. But when we skip the Exploration Stage, we trade revelation for reaction. We move quickly but shallowly. We end up doing good things that may not be *God* things.

Here's why we tend to skip the Exploration Stage:

1. **We're in a hurry.**
   The pressure to "do something" often feels holy, but hurry and holiness rarely travel together.

2. **We equate stillness with weakness.**
   Many leaders feel guilty for slowing down, as though reflection is laziness. In reality, stillness is strength.

3. **We fear what God might actually say.**
   Honest listening can expose uncomfortable truths. It may challenge cherished traditions or reveal painful realities. But truth always precedes transformation.

The Exploration Stage requires courage—the courage to stop talking, stop fixing, and let God speak.

How to Begin the Exploration Stage

Here are practical ways churches (and associations) can begin the Exploration Stage journey:

1. **Call the people to prayer.**
   Promote corporate prayer using a printed daily prayer

guide. Also, establish prayer gatherings where the single agenda is, *"Lord, what are you saying to us?"*

2. Ask spiritual questions.
- *What do we sense God doing in our midst?*
- *What do we celebrate that reflects His presence?*
- *Where have we drifted from His mission?*
- *What breaks our heart that also breaks His?*

3. Listen to your community.
Walk your neighborhoods. Talk with local leaders. Ask what they see and feel. God often speaks through the voices of those outside our walls.

4. Read the Word together.
Choose passages of renewal—Ezra, Nehemiah, Acts, Revelation 2-3—and ask, *"What do we hear for ourselves?"*

5. Document impressions.
Write down recurring themes, Scriptures, or words that surface in prayer. Patterns often reveal the Spirit's fingerprints.

The Exploration Stage is not about gathering conclusions—it's about noticing divine clues.

What Happens During the Exploration Stage

When a church or association commits to the Exploration Stage, three things usually happen:

1. **The atmosphere shifts.**
   Conversations move from complaint to curiosity.
   Instead of *"Who's to blame?"* people begin asking, *"What is God saying?"*

2. **Unity deepens.**
   Prayer creates alignment. People who rarely agreed in meetings often find unexpected harmony when they're listening together.

3. **Hope awakens.**
   The Exploration Stage reminds everyone that God is not done speaking—and if He's still speaking, He's still working.

I've seen congregations on the edge of despair come alive simply because they began to listen.

A Lesson on Spiritual Focus

Oftentimes, renewal teams struggle with direction. Meetings can become tense, even causing trust to erode. Everyone has a different idea of what "renewal" means.

So instead of launching a task force or forming another committee, I begin each meeting with Scripture related to renewal. No conversations are to be had about business, or planning—just Scripture reading and prayer. Practicing this leads to healthy shifts.

People who haven't been speaking kindly to one another begin praying for each other by name. When we meet, we don't start with an agenda—we start with Scripture, prayer, and sharing what they hear God saying. Such a gathering doesn't produce a quick plan. However, it does produce something better: peace. And when ideas and direction came, they were clear and unified.

An effective Exploration Stage does what debate cannot—it aligns hearts before aligning strategy.

The Role of the Leader in the Exploration Stage

The leader's job in this stage is to **guard the atmosphere** of listening. That means resisting the urge to jump ahead. Leaders model the Exploration Stage by asking questions rather than giving answers.

They say things like,
"What do you sense God saying?"
"What Scriptures have been speaking to you lately?"
"Where do you see His hand at work among us?"

This posture invites participation and humility. It reminds everyone that renewal doesn't begin with a boardroom—it begins in a prayer room.

The healthiest Exploration Stages are not led by experts but by *seekers*.

The Exploration Stage and the Holy Spirit

If you listen closely in the early stages of renewal, you'll often sense what I call the *gentle wind*—the subtle but unmistakable movement of the Holy Spirit. It's not dramatic or loud; it's often quiet, like a whisper in the soul.

That's why the Exploration Stage must be spiritual before it becomes strategic. The Spirit leads differently than we plan. He surprises us, redirects us, and sometimes even slows us down so that He can prepare hearts before He gives clarity.

When leaders try to move faster than the Spirit, they risk building what God never blessed. But when they move in rhythm with Him, renewal flows naturally. The Exploration Stage teaches us that the Spirit doesn't just bless our direction—He *is* our direction.

What to Avoid During the Exploration Stage

The Exploration Stage can easily be derailed if leaders aren't careful. Here are three common mistakes:

1. Turning it into an analysis too soon.

The Exploration Stage is about hearing, not solving. Resist the temptation to collect data before you've collected direction.

2. Rushing through silence.

The best insights often come after long pauses. Learn to be comfortable with quiet rooms and waiting hearts.

3. Ignoring uncomfortable promptings.

Sometimes the Spirit surfaces painful truths—a relationship that needs reconciliation, a ministry that needs release, or a sin that needs repentance. Don't silence conviction; it's often the first sign of life.

The goal of the Exploration Stage is not comfort—it's clarity.

The Gift of the Exploration Stage

The Exploration Stage is a gift because it brings leaders back to a state of dependence. It reminds us that renewal is not our idea—it's God's.

When a church or association enters this stage, hope rises, unity deepens, and hearts begin to soften. People start to remember that God truly speaks to His people—not just through sermons or strategies, but through His living presence among them.

Before revival happens in the sanctuary,
    it happens in the soul.
Before clarity comes to the boardroom,
    it comes to the prayer room.
Before churches or associations act,
    they must listen.

That's what makes the Exploration Stage spiritually special. It's the art of waiting for God to breathe.

4 Action Steps of the Exploration Stage

The Exploration Stage is shaped by four essential steps: the **Introduction**, the **Prayer Focus**, the **Member Meetings**, and the **Vital Signs Assessment**. Each step plays a unique role in helping a church or association listen well before leading forward. The most critical work of this stage happens not in planning meetings, but in quiet moments of prayer, storying, and listening.

Together, these four steps form the foundation of the Exploration Stage—anchoring the Renewal Process in prayerful discovery and spiritual readiness.

Action Step 1: The Introduction
The **Introduction** identifies the structure for the entire renewal process. It is the moment the Renewal Leader presents the vision, purpose, and pathway of renewal to the congregation or association. This step emphasizes that

renewal is not a quick fix, but a spiritual journey led by the Holy Spirit. The goal is to inspire hope, invite participation, and foster a shared understanding of why the process is important.

When clearly communicated and prayerfully launched, the Introduction builds anticipation and trust, helping everyone sense that God is calling the church or association to pause, listen, and prepare for new life.

After the Renewal Process is explained in this action step, consider a vote necessary to officially begin the Renewal Process.

Action Step 2: The Prayer Focus
The Prayer Focus Step postures the church or association in prayer and discernment. It's the spiritual act of creating space to hear what God is already saying.

As a church or association journeys through the Exploration Stage, the people are encouraged to engage in a planned season of prayer—no agenda, no voting, no debating. Just prayer and listening. Because when the pace slows, the Spirit speaks.

As a prayer focus resource for churches, the Kentucky Baptist Convention offers a *40-Day Prayer Guide for Church Revitalization*—a valuable prayer focus resource to help congregations seek God's direction in prayer together.

As a prayer focus resource for associations, a 7 Day Prayer guide titled *Praying for My Association* is available by request. (*Note: To receive a copy of the Associational Prayer Guide, simply scan the Free Renewal Resource Kit's QR Code located on page 195 of this book.*)

The question is not *"Do we have a vision?"* but *"Do we have ears to hear what God is saying?"*

Action Step 3: The Membership Meetings

Membership Meetings are a vital part of the Renewal Process, providing the entire church or association with opportunities to share stories of their experiences. These gatherings foster transparency, trust, and unity. Each 45-minute meeting with 5-9 people in small groups is an opportunity to hear their stories through a set of questions. (*Note: To receive a copy of the questions, simply scan the Free Renewal Resource Kit's QR Code located on page 195 of this book.*)

When the people sense that renewal is not just a leadership initiative but a shared spiritual journey, momentum builds, hearts align, and the church or association begins to move forward together in faith and hope.

Action Step 4: **The Vital Signs Assessment (Scorecard)**
The Vital Signs Scorecard is a spiritual and organizational health check for the church or association. It helps the Renewal Team evaluate key areas. By scoring, leaders can identify patterns that reveal growth, stagnation, or decline. More importantly, the Scorecard invites prayerful reflection—helping leaders see beyond the numbers to the spiritual vitality they represent. When used with humility and faith, the Vital Signs Scorecard becomes a tool, not a judgment, but a guide toward renewed mission and ministry health. (*Note: To receive a copy of the Vital Signs Assessment (Scorecard), simply scan the Free Renewal Resource Kit's QR Code located on page 195 of this book.*)

A Leader's Prayer

Lord, teach us to listen again.
Quiet the noise of our plans and opinions.
Help us to hear the still, small voice of Your Spirit.
Reveal what You are already doing in our midst.
Awaken our hearts to Your presence.
Give us the courage to wait until You speak, and humility to obey when You do.

Reflection Questions

1. What practices could help your team slow down and listen to God together?

2. What voices (fear, pressure, urgency) most often drown out the Spirit's whisper in your context?

3. How would your leadership change if you began every new initiative by asking, *"What is God saying?"*

4. What signs might confirm God is stirring renewal among your people right now?

Closing Thought

When leaders in churches and associations humble themselves to ask, *"What is God saying?"*, heaven leans in to answer. And once the answer begins to come, the rest of the process—examination, presentation, recommendation, affirmation, and implementation—unfolds with divine rhythm.

Before the bones come together, before the breath enters, before the plan takes shape—someone must listen.

Knowing When to Move Forward

Exploration is not complete when all voices have spoken. It is complete when **patterns begin to emerge,** and leaders share a growing sense of understanding.

Signs that Exploration is bearing fruit include:
- Increased honesty in conversations.

- Shared language begins to form.
- Reduced urgency for immediate solutions.
- Greater trust among leaders.

Only when these signs are present should leaders consider narrowing the funnel and moving into the next stage, the Examination Stage.

Questions to Ask Before Proceeding

Before proceeding, leaders should pause and ask together:
- *Have we listened without defending?*
- *Are we hearing themes rather than isolated complaints?*
- *Do we share a growing understanding of our reality?*
- *Are we willing to let these insights shape the next stage?*

If the answer is yes, the journey may continue.

Next Chapter: The Examination Stage

The next chapter is the **Examination Stage**. It includes looking deeper, gathering facts, stories, and data that reveal both strengths to celebrate and challenges to confront on the path toward renewal.

CHAPTER FOUR

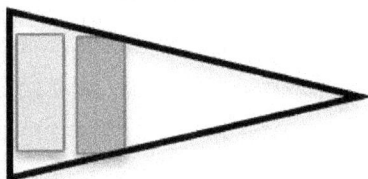

Stage 2
Examination
Knowing Where We Are

2 Corinthians 13:5*a*
"Examine yourselves to see if you are in the faith...."

Examination is the discipline of looking honestly at reality.

After the wide listening of Exploration, leaders may feel both encouraged and unsettled. Stories have been heard. Themes have surfaced. Questions are clearer, but answers remain elusive. Examination provides the next faithful step—not by rushing toward solutions, but by seeking understanding grounded in truth.

Welcome to the **Examination Stage**. This stage asks a different question than Exploration.

Part II: The Six-Stage Process

If the Exploration Stage begins by asking *"What is God saying?"*, the Examination Stage begins by asking *"Where are we now?"*

One of the most difficult and sacred tasks of leadership is facing reality. Before any vision can take root, we must first tell the truth about the present. The Examination Stage is not criticism—it's clarity. It's the second stage of the Funnel Graph, where the wide openness of the Exploration Stage begins to take shape through honest reflection.

In this stage, leaders seek to understand not just what God is saying, but what condition His people are in. It's where prayer meets perspective. The Exploration Stage reveals God's voice; the Examination Stage reveals our reality.

The Purpose of Examination

The purpose of Examination is **clarity through assessment**. It seeks to understand the current condition of the church or association by examining the data, culture, systems, demographics, and practices alongside stories gathered earlier.

Examination is not about proving decline or defending success. It is about aligning perception with reality. When leaders refuse to examine honestly, assumptions quietly take over. When leaders examine humbly, clarity grows.

This stage narrows the funnel by replacing impressions with insight.

The Courage to See Clearly

It's easier to dream about the future than to diagnose the present. But every movement of the renewal begins when leaders are willing to see things as they really are, not as they wish they were.

Jesus modeled this perfectly in Revelation 2-3 when He addressed the seven churches. To each one, He spoke commendation and correction. He didn't flatter them, and He didn't condemn them. He simply told the truth in love.

That's the spirit of the Examination Stage. It's not about fault-finding; it's about truth-telling. Because truth, even when painful, is always the first step toward freedom.

Leaders who avoid honest examination often remain trapped in cycles of denial. They repeat the same patterns, defend the same traditions, and wonder why nothing changes. But those who embrace examination discover that truth is not their enemy—it's their ally.

Moving from Stories to Stewardship

The stories heard during Exploration are essential, but they are incomplete without examination. Stories reveal experience; examination reveals patterns.

This stage helps leaders steward the information entrusted to them. It asks leaders to consider:
- What the data confirms
- What the data challenges.
- What the data complicates.

Examination does not diminish lived experience. It deepens understanding by placing it within a broader context.

What Should Be Examined

While every context is unique, faithful examination typically includes four interconnected areas.

1. Spiritual and Missional Health
Leaders examine faithfulness to mission, clarity of gospel witness, prayer life, disciple-making practices, and alignment with biblical calling.

2. Cultural and Relational Dynamics
This includes trust levels, conflict patterns, communication habits, leadership health, and the unspoken norms shaping behavior.

3. Organizational and Structural Reality
Structures, systems, governance, staffing, decision-making processes, and ministry alignment are examined for effectiveness and sustainability.

4. Demographic and Community Context
Leaders consider who they are reaching, who they are not, how the surrounding community has changed, and whether the church or association reflects its mission field.

Each area should be approached with curiosity, not critique.

Why the Examination Stage is So Important

In this second stage of the Renewal Process, clarity deepens. While the Exploration Stage is largely spiritual—listening, discerning, and praying—the Examination Stage is both spiritual and practical. It involves gathering data, studying patterns, and asking hard questions.

Here's why it matters:

1. You cannot lead from where you aren't.
Vision disconnected from reality becomes fantasy. Until you know where you are, you can't know where to go.

2. Truth creates trust.
People follow leaders who are honest, even about uncomfortable realities. When you name what everyone else senses, but no one has said, credibility grows.

3. Accurate diagnosis prevents wasted effort.
Without examination, churches or associations may

69

treat symptoms instead of causes—fixing attendance when the deeper issue is discipleship, or chasing relevance when the real need is repentance.

4. Clarity honors God.
He is the God of truth. When leaders tell the truth, they reflect His character.

Examination is discipleship. It's the practice of bringing everything into the light so that God can heal what's broken.

How to Conduct a Spiritual Examination

There are many ways to examine a church or association, but the healthiest processes are *prayerful, participatory, and practical.* Here are some guiding steps:

1. Pray for the Spirit's illumination.
Before collecting information, invite the Spirit to reveal what numbers cannot. Ask Him to show blind spots and hidden strengths.

2. Use multiple lenses.
Gather insights through surveys, interviews, and group discussions. Examine worship attendance, community engagement, finances, leadership structures, and discipleship pathways.

3. Ask courageous questions.

- *What is truly bearing fruit, and what is simply keeping us busy?*
- *What ministries no longer serve our mission?*
- *Where are people growing spiritually, and where are they stagnating?*
- *How are we known in our community?*
- *What do our leaders need most from us right now?*

4. Look for patterns, not just points.

One person's opinion is an anecdote; then similar responses are a pattern. Patterns reveal priorities.

5. Listen deeply, respond slowly.

Don't rush to conclusions. Let the findings speak for themselves before reacting emotionally.

Examination works best when it is seen not as a threat, but as a gift—a mirror God holds up to help us see what He already knows.

A Biblical Model for Examination

In Numbers 13, Moses sent twelve men to explore the Promised Land. Their task was simple: *"See what the land is like."* They were to observe, record, and report. That's examination.

But when they returned, ten of them saw only problems, while two—Joshua and Caleb saw potential. The difference wasn't the data; it was in the interpretation.

That's why examination must be done through faith. Seeing clearly doesn't mean losing hope. The purpose of examination is not to depress God's people—it's to prepare them.

Joshua and Caleb proved that honesty and hope can coexist. You can face hard truths without losing sight of God's promises.

What Examination Reveals

When churches and associations commit to honest examination, they usually discover three kinds of truths:

1. Encouraging Truths:
Evidence of God's faithfulness—stories of growth, unity, and lives changed. These remind the people that renewal begins from grace, not guilt.

2. Painful Truths:
Areas of decline, division, or drift. These often surface unspoken frustrations, but when addressed with humility, they become catalysts for healing.

3. Surprising Truths:

New opportunities or strengths that no one noticed before. Sometimes examination reveals resources and relationships that have been overlooked.

The goal is to see all three clearly. If you only look for strengths, you'll become complacent. If you only look for weaknesses, you'll become discouraged. Balanced examination keeps both in view.

The Role of the Examination Leader

Leaders set the tone for honest examination. Their attitude will determine whether people engage or retreat.

A wise leader says:

"We're not looking for blame—we're looking for understanding."

"This isn't about judgment—it's about growth."

"We can't fix what we won't face, but we can face anything together with grace."

Leaders must model vulnerability. When a pastor admits, *"We've lost some momentum,"* or when an associational leader says, *"We haven't been as unified as we could be,"* it opens the door for honesty across the organization.

The leader who tells the truth gives everyone else permission to do the same.

The Posture Required for Examination Leaders

Examination requires courage—but not combativeness.

Leaders must resist the temptation to defend their legacy or minimize concerns. They must also resist the urge to assign blame. Examination is not an audit of faithfulness or a referendum on past leadership. It is an act of stewardship for the future.

The guiding posture is humility: a willingness to learn what is true, even when it is uncomfortable.

Turning Facts into Faith

Examination is not the end—it's preparation for what comes next. The goal is not to gather data for data's sake, but to discern God's direction through what the data reveals.

When you look honestly at your current condition, you must interpret it through the lens of faith. God never exposes without the intent to restore.

As Job recorded, *"He wounds, but He also binds up; He shatters, but His hands heal."* (Job 5:18). The same hands that uncover also redeem.

When churches discover painful realities—decline, division, drift—they should remember that conviction is evidence of

74

God's nearness, not His absence. It's His way of saying, *"I love you too much to let you stay where you are."*

Common Pitfalls of Examination

1. Blame Shifting:

Pointing fingers at past leaders or certain groups only deepens wounds. Remember: you're not looking for villains; you're seeking vision.

2. Data Overload:

Too much information without interpretation leads to paralysis. Focus on the key insights that matter most.

3. Defensiveness:

Some will resist change by defending "the way we've always done it." Gently remind them that the goal is faithfulness, not fault-finding.

4. Hopelessness:

Don't let sobering truths turn into despair. Every challenge is an invitation to trust God anew.

Examination without grace wounds. Grace without examination withers. Healthy renewal requires both. When examination feels threatening, leaders should slow down and revisit posture before proceeding.

The Fruit of Examination

When done prayerfully, the Examination Stage produces three vital results:

1. Humility.
Seeing ourselves accurately softens our hearts and renews our dependence on God.

2. Clarity.
The fog begins to lift. Leaders can see where God is inviting transformation.

3. Readiness.
The congregation becomes emotionally and spiritually prepared for the next stage—**Presentation**, where findings are shared openly and direction begins to form.

The Examination Stage clears the ground for new growth. You cannot plant renewal in denial.

Sharing Findings with Integrity

Examination is not complete until findings are shared honestly and carefully among leaders. Transparency builds trust, but timing and tone matter.

Leaders should:
- Share findings clearly.

- Avoid dramatizing or minimizing.
- Frame insights within prayer and purpose.
- Allow time for processing.

This sharing is internal. Public communication comes later in the process. At this stage, clarity among leaders matters more than consensus among the congregation.

Tools That Serve the Examination Stage

While Exploration relies on open conversation, Examination often involves structured tools. These tools may include:
- Health assessments.
- Attendance and participation trends.
- Financial patterns.
- Leadership and member surveys.
- Ministry inventories.
- Community demographic data.

Tools serve the process only when interpreted prayerfully and communally. Numbers do not tell the whole story, but they tell part of it—and ignoring them weakens discernment.

3 Action Steps of the Examination Stage

In the **Examination Stage**, the church or association looks carefully at its present reality. It's about understanding what is true today, so that wise, Spirit-led decisions can be made tomorrow. It is built around three essential steps: the **Church Information**, **Community Demographics**, and the **Leadership Questionnaire.**

Together, these three steps provide a balanced view—what's happening inside, what's happening around, and what leaders are sensing. This honest examination prepares the church or association to hear what God may be saying next.

Action Step 1: **The Church Information Step**
The Church Information Step provides a clear snapshot of the church's current reality. During this step, the Renewal Team gathers essential facts—membership numbers, attendance patterns, financial reports, and ministry activities. This data helps the team see where the church has been, where it is, and where God may be leading. It is not about judgment, but about clarity—understanding the story the numbers tell. When prayerfully interpreted, this information becomes a mirror reflecting both strengths to celebrate and areas needing renewal, helping leaders make informed, Spirit-led decisions about the church or association's future. *(Source: Annual Church Profile—available from local association, network, state convention, or denomination.)*

Action Step 2: **The Community Demographics Step**
The Community Demographics Step helps the church (or association) understand the people and context it is called to reach. By studying population trends, age groups, income levels, education, and cultural diversity, the Renewal Team

gains insight into the mission field right outside its doors. This step reveals how the surrounding community (typically a 1-3-5-10-mile radius or an entire county) is changing and where ministry opportunities are emerging. It challenges assumptions, opens eyes, and invites fresh compassion for neighbors who may not yet know Christ. When viewed through prayerful discernment, demographic data becomes more than numbers—it becomes a map guiding the church toward renewed, contextualized mission. *(Sources: local association, network, state convention, or census bureau.)*

Action Step 3: **The Leadership Questionnaire Step**
The Leadership Questionnaire Step invites the voices of pastors, staff, and key lay leaders into the renewal journey. Through a thoughtfully designed set of questions, leaders share their honest perception about their church or association's strengths, challenges, and spiritual health. This step values perception over perfection. The collected responses help the Renewal Team discern themes, identify barriers, and recognize areas of communication needs. *(Note: To receive a copy of the questionnaire, simply scan the Free Renewal Resource Kit's QR Code located on page 195 of this book.)*

A Leader's Prayer

Lord, give us courage to see what You already see.
Help us face the truth with humility,
not fear.

Where we've grown complacent,
awaken us.
Where we've drifted, draw us back.
Where we've lost our way,
lead us home.
Teach us that honesty is not defeat—it's the doorway to
hope.
May our examination glorify You by preparing us for Your
renewal.

Reflection Questions

1. What truths about your church or association have you been hesitant to face?

2. How might honest examination strengthen trust among your leaders and members?

3. What practical tools could you use to assess your current health and mission effectiveness?

4. In what ways has God used past moments of truth to bring new growth in your community?

Closing Thoughts

Examination is not a valley of shame—it's a hallway of grace. It's where God's people stop pretending and start progressing. When a church finally says, *"Here's where we really are,"* heaven leans in with mercy.

This second stage of the Renewal Process reminds us that truth is not the enemy of faith—it's the soil in which faith grows.

Knowing When to Move Forward

Examination has served its purpose when leaders can articulate:

- A shared understanding of current reality.
- Areas of strength to steward.
- Areas of misalignment to address.
- Questions that remain unanswered.

At this point, the funnel narrows again—not toward decisions, but toward clarity.

The next stage will focus on **Presentation**—communicating what has been learned in a way that is truthful, careful, and constructive.

Questions to Ask Before Proceeding

Before proceeding, leaders should pause and ask:

- *Are we aligned in our understanding of reality?*
- *Have we examined without blame or fear?*

- *Are we willing to share what we have learned honestly?*
- *Do we trust the process enough to move forward together?*

If the answer is yes, the journey may continue.

Examination does not tell leaders what to do. It tells them what is true. And truth, handled with humility, prepares the way for discernment.

Next Chapter: The Presentation Stage

The next chapter is the **Presentation Stage**, which transforms what has been learned into a presentation of stories (report) and possibilities (recommendations).

CHAPTER FIVE

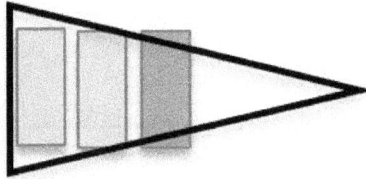

Stage Three
Presentation
Sharing the Vision with Others

"...and my speech and my message were not in plausible words of wisdom, but in demonstration of the Spirit and of the power, so that your faith might not rest in the wisdom of men but in the power of God."—1 Corinthians 2:4-5

Presentation is the discipline of telling the truth with clarity and care.

After listening widely and examining honestly, leaders now face a critical responsibility: how to communicate what has been learned. Presentation is not about persuading people toward a decision or managing reactions. It is about **sharing reality faithfully**, in a way that invites understanding rather than fear.

Welcome to the **Presentation Stage**. This stage asks a different question than the previous two.

Exploration asks, *What are we hearing?*
Examination asks, *What is true?*
Presentation asks, *How do we share the truth so that it can be received?*

When leaders have taken the time to **explore what God is saying** and **examine their own position**, the next essential step is to **share what they have discovered**. Renewal is never a private revelation; it becomes powerful only when it is shared with the people who will live it out.

This is the **Presentation Stage** of the Renewal Process—the spiritual moment when discernment gives way to dialogue, and clarity begins to spread throughout the body.

The Purpose of the Presentation Stage

The purpose of Presentation is **shared understanding**.

Until this point, clarity has been forming primarily among leaders. Presentation widens the circle again—not to restart exploration, but to invite others into the reality that has been discerned. When done well, Presentation builds trust. When rushed or mishandled, it can undo the work of earlier stages.

Presentation narrows the funnel by replacing speculation with shared clarity.

Why the Presentation Stage Matters

The Presentation Stage bridges the gap between *discovery* and *direction*. Without it, renewal remains an idea trapped in a small circle of leaders. With it, the whole body begins to see the same reality, feel the same burden, and anticipate the same future.

Leaders who skip this stage often wonder why others don't feel the same urgency they do. The reason is simple: people can't follow a vision they haven't yet seen.

The presentation included in the Presentation Stage is not about making a speech—it's about creating shared understanding. It's less about performance and more about participation.

From Private Clarity to Public Conversation

Up to this point in the Renewal Process, much of the work has been private: prayer, surveys, conversations, and information gathering. Now, it moves into the open.

In the Presentation Stage, the task is to communicate what's been learned in a way that is honest, hopeful, and clear. It's not the moment to defend findings or demand action—it's the moment to invite others to see what you've seen.

Effective presentations help people move from *awareness* to *alignment*. It answers three key questions that every listener has in their heart:
1. What did we learn?
2. What does it mean?
3. What might God be calling us to do next?

If those questions are answered clearly and humbly, the Spirit will do the rest.

The Responsibility of Truth-Telling

Truth-telling in renewal work is both necessary and pastoral. Leaders are called to be honest without being harsh, clear without being cold, and transparent without being reckless. This requires discipline.

Presentation should:
- Reflect what was actually heard and examined.
- Avoid exaggeration or minimization.
- Distinguish facts from interpretations.
- Honor the voices of those who contributed.

The goal is not to convince everyone to agree, but to ensure that everyone understands the same reality.

The Spiritual Posture of Presentation

Presentation is a spiritual act before it is a leadership task. It requires humility and transparency. You're not announcing what *you* discovered—you're sharing what *God* revealed. That distinction changes the tone entirely. The leader's posture should echo what Jesus said in John 7:16: *"My teaching is not mine, but He who sent me."*

When you present that with humility, people sense authenticity. They're more likely to listen because they recognize that you're not pushing an agenda; you're communicating discernment.

The spirit of the presentation in the Presentation Stage is:
- **Gentle, not defensive.**
- **Honest, not harsh.**
- **Hopeful, not naïve**

Renewal spreads through truth wrapped in grace.

How to Prepare for the Presentation

Preparing for the Presentation is more than organizing information; it's about preparing hearts to communicate God's direction with clarity and grace. Use this opportunity to call for unity among leaders, to offer a thoughtful message, and to foster a prayerful spirit.

Part II: The Six-Stage Process

1. Clarify the message.

Before speaking publicly, summarize the key insights from the Examination Stage. Narrow the findings to a few clear themes—ideally three to five. People remember patterns, not paragraphs.

2. Pray over the tone.

Ask God to prepare your heart and the hearts of the listeners. The goal is not to impress but to invite.

3. Anticipate emotions.

Some will feel affirmed; others may feel anxious or even defensive. Prepare to respond with patience and empathy.

4. Choose the right setting.

Presentation should happen in a setting that involves dialogue. This might be a town-hall-style meeting, a leadership retreat, or a combined worship service.

5. Use visuals wisely.

Charts, stories, and testimonies help people see what they're hearing. A simple Funnel Graph diagram can help communicate where the group is in the process.

6. End with invitation, not conclusion.

Don't rush to solutions. Close by asking, *"What stands out to you?"* or *"What do you sense God saying to us through this?"*

Presentation should plant seeds, not settle arguments.

Who Should Hear What—and When

Not every detail belongs in every setting. Wisdom is required to determine **who hears what, and when**. Typically:

- **Key leaders** receive the fullest level of detail.
- **Congregations or broader groups** receive a synthesized, accessible summary.
- **Sensitive information** is handled carefully and appropriately.

This is not secrecy. It is stewardship. Trust is preserved when leaders communicate with integrity and discernment.

How to Present Findings Faithfully

Effective Presentation is guided by several principles.

1. Begin with Purpose
Frame the presentation within prayer and mission. Remind people *why* this process is happening and *what faithfulness looks like* at this stage.

2. Use Clear, Shared Language
Avoid technical jargon or insider language. Speak plainly. Clarity builds confidence.

3. Name Both Strengths and Challenges
Faithful presentation resists extremes. It acknowledges what is life-giving while also naming what is misaligned.

4. Avoid Premature Solutions
This is not the time to propose change. Presentation creates understanding, not decisions.

5. Allow Space for Processing
Silence, questions, and emotional responses are part of the work. Resist the urge to fill every gap.

The Role of Storytelling

Facts inform the mind, but stories move the heart. Every effective presentation includes both. While data and observations bring clarity, stories bring connection. They remind listeners that renewal isn't theoretical—it's personal.

When sharing findings, include testimonials from the Exploration and Examination Stages:
- A member who felt God stirring their heart in prayer.
- A community partner who noticed the church's kindness.
- A moment when the team saw God's fingerprints in the process.

Stories anchor truth in emotion. They help people see themselves in the narrative of renewal.

A Biblical Model: Nehemiah's Presentation

After surveying the ruins of Jerusalem, Nehemiah gathered the people and said,

"You see the trouble we are in...Come, let us rebuild the wall of Jerusalem, and we will no longer be in disgrace." (Nehemiah 2:17)

He didn't exaggerate or minimize. He simply told the truth: *"You see the trouble we are in."* Then he invited participation: *"Come, let us rebuild."*

Notice the balance—honest reality combined with hopeful invitation. That's the heart of an effective presentation.

Nehemiah's presentation was short, clear, and Spirit-filled. It transformed a discouraged crowd into a unified movement. That's what happens when truth is communicated with humility and faith.

Emotional Dynamics of the Presentation Stage

When new insights are presented, people respond emotionally before they respond logically. Some will feel relief—finally, someone has named what they've been sensing. Others will feel threatened—change often triggers fear. Still others will feel energized—the Spirit is confirming what they already hoped.

Wise leaders expect all three reactions. They listen more than they lecture. They acknowledge tension but don't let it define the moment. A helpful phrase during this stage is: *"Thank you for sharing that. Let's keep listening to what God is saying through one another."* That response disarms defensiveness and keeps the focus on discernment, not debate.

How to Handle Resistance

Resistance is not failure—it's feedback. It simply means people care deeply about the future. Think on these things when you encounter pushback during the Presentation Stage:

1. Stay calm.
Don't argue. Listen. People aren't rejecting you—they're processing change.

2. Affirm emotions.
"I understand this feels hard. Thank you for being honest."

3. Refocus on mission.
"We're all here because we love this church (or association) and want to see it healthy again."

4. Leave space for prayer.
Invite the Spirit to soften hearts and confirm truth.

Over time, transparency builds trust. The very people who resist early often become advocates later.

Common Pitfalls in the Presentation Stage

1. Overloading with information.
Too many details overwhelm. Keep it simple and visual.

2. Skipping emotion.
Facts without empathy feel cold. Connect spiritually and relationally.

3. Demanding agreement.
The goal is awareness, not immediate consensus. Unity comes later.

4. Neglecting follow-up.
Always provide a way for people to respond, such as discussion sessions, feedback forms, or prayer gatherings.

Your presentation is not the end of communication; it's the beginning of a conversation.

The Role of the Leader in Presentation Stage

In the Presentation Stage, the leader acts as a translator—converting spiritual insights into a shared language. You're helping people understand:
- **What God is revealing.**

- **Why it matters.**
- **How it connects to their lives.**

Leaders who communicate with clarity and humility help congregations see that renewal is not something being *done to them*—it's something God is *doing among them.*

Transitioning from the Presentation Stage to the Recommendation Stage

The Presentation Stage is not about making decisions—it's about creating readiness.

When it's done well, people begin to ask new questions:
- *"So, what do we do next?"*
- *"How do we address what we've learned?"*
- *"What steps would help us follow through?"*

Those questions signal that the group is ready to move to the next stage: **Recommendation.**

Don't rush prematurely. Let the insights of the Presentation Stage settle. Allow time for conversation, prayer, and confirmation.

When hearts are united around truth, direction will emerge naturally.

2 Action Steps of the Presentation Stage

The **Presentation Stage** marks a pivotal moment in the Renewal Process. What has been learned through prayer, exploration, and examination now begins to take visible shape. This stage moves the Renewal Team from gathering information to sharing insight and direction with the church or association. The goal is not to simply report findings, but to communicate them in a way that invites unity, faith, and forward movement.

This stage includes two key steps: **the Written Report** and **the Proposed Recommendations.** *Note: Both the Written Report and the Proposed Recommendations should first be presented to the Renewal Team by the Renewal Leader in draft form before they are finalized and shared with the public.*

Action Step 1: Written Report

The Written Report serves as a bridge between discovery and direction. Compiled by the Renewal Team (and written by the Renewal Leader), it summarizes the key findings of the Exploration and Examination Stages in clear, factual, and faith-filled language. The report highlights patterns, strengths, and opportunities revealed through prayer, data, and discussion. Its purpose is not to criticize but to clarify— to help the church or association to see itself honestly through both spiritual and practical lenses. When presented with humility and hope, the Written Report becomes a powerful tool that invites understanding, builds trust, and invites the church or association to the next step in the renewal process: the recommendations.

Action Step 2: Proposed Recommendations
The Proposed Recommendations translate what has been learned into a clear, prayerfully discerned path forward. Developed by the Renewal Team under the guidance of the Holy Spirit, these recommendations outline practical and spiritual steps that can move the church or association toward greater health and mission effectiveness. Each recommendation should reflect both faith and wisdom—rooted in biblical principles and shaped by what has been discovered through the process. Presented with humility and clarity, these proposed actions—typically categorized into four areas: leadership, administration, ministry, and mission—invite the church or association to respond together, trusting that God is revealing not just what needs to change, but also how genuine renewal can begin.

Note: To receive a copy of a Sample Report & Recommendations, simply scan the Free Renewal Resource Kit's QR Code located on page 195 of this book.

A Leader's Prayer

Lord, teach me to speak with both truth and grace.
Help me communicate not to impress, but to invite.

*Give me wisdom to share what You've revealed with
humility and hope.
Prepare hearts to receive Your direction.
May our words be instruments of unity and clarity,
and may everything we say lead people closer to You.*

Reflection Questions

1. How can you communicate discoveries from the first two stages in a way that builds trust and unity?

2. What fears or tensions might surface during presentation, and how can you address them with grace?

3. Who could share personal stories that help make the message more relatable and real?

4. What next step could you plan to keep the conversation going after the initial presentation?

Closing Thought

The Presentation Stage is the hinge of the Renewal Process —the turning point where prayer and truth become a shared purpose. When leaders communicate with humility and courage, walls fall and bridges form. The Spirit begins knitting hearts together around God's direction.

Before action can be unified, understanding must be shared. That's what happens here. When the people begin to see what the leaders have seen—and believe that God Himself has spoken—renewal is no longer a theory. It's about to become a movement.

At this point, the funnel narrows again. The next stage will not yet call for action, but for discernment—clarifying possible pathways forward.

Questions to Ask Before Proceeding

Before proceeding, leaders should pause and ask:
- *Have we told the truth clearly and carefully?*
- *Have we honored both people and reality?*
- *Have we resisted the urge to rush ahead?*
- *Are we prepared to walk patiently with those still processing?*

If the answer is yes, the journey may continue.

Next Chapter: The Affirmation Stage

The next chapter, the **Affirmation Stage**, focuses on unity— bringing the body together to pray, discuss, and confirm the path ahead. It is here that faith deepens, trust strengthens, and the church collectively says, *"Yes, Lord, we will follow where you lead.*

CHAPTER SIX

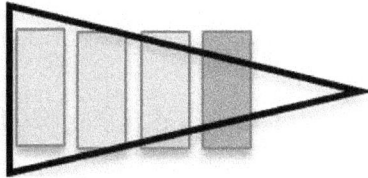

Stage 4
Recommendation
"Discerning the Way Forward"

"Trust in the Lord with all your heart, and do not lean on your own understanding. In all your ways acknowledge him, and he will make your paths straight."—Proverbs 3:5-6

Every journey of renewal eventually reaches a turning point—a moment when leaders must move from *listening* to *leading*, from *discovering* to *deciding*. That moment is the Recommendation Stage of the Renewal Process.

Welcome to the **Recommendation Stage**. This is where vision begins to take shape and hope becomes a plan.

Up to this point, the church or association has prayed, listened, and examined honestly. They've shared findings transparently through the Presentation Stage. Now, they begin to ask a new question: *"What is God calling us to **do** about what we've learned?"*

The Recommendation Stage is the discipline of discernment.

After truth has been shared and understood, leaders often feel a renewed urgency to act. Questions become sharper. Conversations naturally turn toward the future. This stage provides a faithful way forward—not by rushing to solutions, but by carefully naming **possible pathways** that emerge from what has been learned.

This stage does not ask, *What must we do?*
It asks, *What paths are before us?*

The Purpose of the Recommendation Stage

The Recommendation Stage transforms understanding into action. It's where leaders propose Spirit-guided next steps that help the church or association live out what God has revealed. This stage is not about drafting a detailed strategic plan—it's about defining the direction of obedience.

In practical terms, the Recommendation Stage seeks to answer four key questions:

1. What have we learned that must change?
2. What have we learned that must remain?
3. What new priorities is God calling us to pursue?

4. What first steps can we take to move forward faithfully?

Leaders who take time to prayerfully build recommendations create a bridge between inspiration and implementation.

Who Shapes the Recommendations

Recommendation is primarily the work of a **smaller leadership group**—often a designated Renewal Team, leadership council, or executive team. *(Note: This group is typically formed at the outset of the church or association's decision to engage in the Renewal Process formally. It usually consists of seven members.)* While broader voices have informed the process earlier, this stage requires concentrated discernment.

This does not diminish the importance of earlier participation. It honors it by ensuring that recommendations are formed carefully, prayerfully, and responsibly.

Leaders shaping recommendations should be:
- Trusted.
- Representative.
- Prayerful.
- Willing to hold tension.

The credibility of this stage depends on the integrity of those entrusted with it.

A Biblical Model: Acts 15 and Jerusalem Council

The early church faced one of its greatest challenges in Acts 15: disagreements over how Gentile believers should follow Christ. After much debate, the apostles gathered, prayed, listened, and reached a Spirit-led decision. Their conclusion was summarized in a single phrase:

"It seemed good to the Holy Spirit and to us..." (Acts 15:28)

That statement captures the essence of the Recommendation Stage. The apostles didn't rush to fix the problem: they sought divine clarity. They didn't impose an agenda; they discerned direction. Their recommendations were simple, clear, and Spirit-centered—and they preserved unity in the early church.

That's our goal, too. The best recommendations arise from collaboration between *the Holy Spirit* and *God's people.*

The Spiritual Posture of Recommendation Stage

The temptation in this stage is to shift from discernment to control. After all, leaders love action—we want to see results! But if this process becomes purely managerial, we risk losing the spiritual heart of the journey.

The right posture is prayerful confidence—firm but flexible, decisive but dependent.

Stage 4: Recommendation, *Discerning the Way Forward*

A good leader in this stage will say, *"Here's what we believe God is showing us, and we are willing to take the first step."*

It's not a dictation of plans—it's an *invitation* to obedience.

How to Develop Recommendations

Developing practical recommendations requires both discernment and clarity. They should be realistic, Spirit-led, and aligned with the mission of the church or association. Leaders can provide a pathway that inspires confidence and moves the body forward together.

Here are six principles:

1. Gather the core insights.

Review all the discoveries from the Exploration, Examination, and Presentation Stages. Identify 3-5 central truths or priorities that consistently surfaced.

2. Name the problem with clarity and grace.

Example: *"Our church has lost focus on reaching our community"* or *"Our association needs clearer communication systems."*

3. Discern the path forward.

Ask, *"If God is calling us to address this, what would obedience look like?"* Keep recommendations clear and concise.

4. Align with mission and Scripture.

Every proposed step should connect directly to biblical principles and the core mission of the church or association.

5. Consider short-term and long-term impact.

Suggest immediate "first steps" that can be started within 90 days and broader goals for one to three years.

6. Pray through each recommendation.

Before presenting them publicly, ask God for unity, humility, and confirmation.

The best recommendations are simple enough to remember, spiritual enough to inspire, and specific enough to act on.

The Characteristics of a God-Honoring Recommendation

A God-honoring recommendation reflects more than good strategy—it reveals the heart of a leader who seeks God's will above personal preference. Such recommendations are prayerfully formed, biblically grounded, and aimed at advancing the mission of Christ's Church. They invite both trust and unity among His people.

A healthy recommendation should be:
- Biblically grounded. It aligns with God's Word, not just good ideas.

- Spirit-led. It reflects prayerful discernment rather than human ambition.
- Mission-focused. It moves the church or association toward its God-given purpose.
- Realistic. It's achievable with available resources and people.
- Collaborative. It invites participation rather than imposing direction.
- Measurable. It allows for progress to be observed and celebrated.

If a recommendation checks these boxes, it's ready to be shared.

Balancing Vision and Practicality

In this part of the Recommendation Stage, leaders must walk a fine line: too much vision without detail leads to confusion; too much detail without vision leads to exhaustion.

The key is to articulate the *WHY* before the *HOW*.

Here is an example:
- **Why (focus):** *"We believe God is calling us to re-engage our community.*
- **How (recommendations):** *"We will begin by adopting one local school and forming a team to serve teachers and families."*

This approach grounds strategy in purpose. It reminds people that the goal isn't just activity—it's alignment with God's heart.

How Recommendations Are Formed

Faithful recommendations emerge through prayer, reflection, and conversation. They are not brainstormed casually or decided hastily.

Effective recommendation development includes:
- Revisiting findings from earlier stages.
- Naming non-negotiables.
- Identifying constraints and capacities.
- Testing options against mission and calling.
- Listening for convergence over time.

Often, clarity emerges gradually rather than suddenly. Leaders should resist the urge to force agreement or finalize language prematurely.

Building Recommendations Collaboratively

While the leadership team often drafts the recommendations, the process should involve others. Invite pastors, staff, and lay leaders to review and refine them. This inclusion builds ownership. When people help shape the plan, they feel part of the journey rather than spectators.

A helpful practice is to host a **Recommendation Gathering**—a half-day gathering where participants pray through discoveries and brainstorm next steps together. These could be called Town Hall Meetings. Out of the conversation, patterns of consensus will emerge.

Remember: collaboration doesn't weaken leadership, it strengthens it.

How to Present Recommendations

Once recommendations are drafted, present them clearly and prayerfully:

- Use simple language—avoid insider terms or complex explanations.
- Provide context: "These steps come from months of prayer, listening, and evaluation.
- Share them visually (slides, handouts, charts).
- Explain how they align with Scripture and the church's or association's mission.
- Invite questions and feedback.
- End with a prayer for unity and obedience.

When people sense humility and transparency, they will respond with trust.

Navigating Challenges in Recommendation Stage

The Recommendation Stage often brings both opportunity and challenge. After careful exploration and examination, leaders must now translate insights into actionable proposals that call for faith, wisdom, and unity. Navigating the challenges helps leaders face the resistance, clarify vision, and guide their people toward courageous, Spirit-led decisions. Here are some of the challenges:

1. Fear of change.

Some will worry that the recommendations threaten cherished tradition. Remind them that honoring the past doesn't mean living in it.

2. Overcomplication.

Avoid recommending too much too fast. Simplicity invites participation.

3. Unrealistic expectation.

Renewal takes time. Be honest about the process—fruit follows faithfulness, not frenzy.

4. Ownership confusion.

Assign clear responsibility. Every recommendation should have a "who" attached to it.

The Renewal Process illustrated using the Funnel Graph narrows here. It's time to define direction.

The Emotional Side of Recommendation Stage

The Recommendation Stage can feel exhilarating and heavy at the same time. Leaders sense excitement about the future but also pressure to "get it right."

Remember this: God blesses faithfulness more than perfection.

The goal isn't to predict everything correctly—it's to move forward obediently. The Spirit can steer a moving vessel much easier than a stationary one.

Courageous leadership means stepping into uncertainty with confidence in God's sovereignty. This stage is especially vulnerable to missteps.

Common pitfalls include:
- Presenting only one "preferred" option.
- Framing recommendations to control outcomes.
- Minimizing the cost of change.
- Overloading recommendations with detail.
- Rushing to a vote or decision.

When this stage is mishandled, trust can fracture quickly. Leaders should slow down rather than speed up when uncertainty rises.

Turning Recommendations into Actions

Once recommendations are shared, allow time for reflection and prayer. Encourage people to test what they've heard against Scripture and their own spiritual discernment.

As consensus forms, the recommendations can become **affirmations**—decisions the body makes together.

2 Steps of the Recommendation Stage

The Recommendation Stage represents a crucial turning point in the Renewal Process. At this point, the Renewal Team has studied, prayed, listened, examined the facts, and confirmed the direction. Now the time has come to communicate the proposed recommendations to the church or association clearly, humbly, and thoughtfully. This stage ensures that members are fully informed and spiritually prepared before moving toward affirmation.

There are two key steps in the Recommendation Stage: Town Hall Meeting #1 and Town Hall Meeting #2. Both Town Hall Meetings are identical in content and purpose, simply offered on two separate dates, so members who are unable to attend one may still participate in the other. Together, these steps help the members move from information to understanding to confidence, while protecting unity and strengthening trust before the Affirmation Stage arrives.

Action Step 1: Town Hall Meeting #1

Town Hall Meeting #1 is the first opportunity for the church or association to hear the Report and the proposed Recommendations in a conversational and supportive environment, even though both have already been made available at least one week prior via hard copy distribution, email, and/or church or association website. During this meeting, the Renewal Leader and the Renewal Team present the Report and the proposed Recommendations in draft form, explaining the purpose behind each one and how they connect to what was discovered earlier in the process and communicated in the Report. Members are encouraged to ask questions, seek understanding, share insights, and offer feedback. This is not a voting meeting, but a listening meeting.

Action Step 2: Town Hall Meeting #2

Town Hall Meeting #2 is identical to Town Hall Meeting #1. It is offered on a different date, so members who are unable to attend one may still participate in the other.

Note: Since the proposed Recommendations are designed to work together toward a single overall objective, they cannot be changed or amended individually on the floor. Any suggested changes must first be brought back to the Renewal Team for prayerful review and possible re-proposal at a later date, which may consequently alter the "vote" date.

A Leader's Prayer

Lord, thank You for the clarity You've given us through this process.
Teach us now to turn revelation into direction.
Keep us from rushing ahead of Your Spirit or lagging behind Your timing.
Please give us the courage to recommend what is right, even when it's difficult.
Unite our hearts around Your will, and let every plan bring You glory.
Make our recommendations pathways of obedience, not monuments of pride.

Reflection Questions

1. What key truths or patterns have surfaced that should shape your recommendations?

2. How can you ensure each proposed step reflects both Scripture and the Spirit's leading?

3. Who should be involved in shaping and refining your recommendations?

4. What short-term and long-term goals should flow from your recommendations?

Closing Thought

Recommendation is where faith meets formation. It's where listening turns into leading and obedience begins to take shape.

The goal is not to craft a perfect plan but to discern the next faithful step.

When God's people seek His direction together and move forward in unity, the Funnel Graph narrows—not to restrict, but to focus.

As the church or association begins to act on what God has shown, renewal stops being an idea and starts becoming a reality.

Knowing When to Move Forward

Before recommendations are shared broadly, leaders should ensure:
- Language is clear and accessible.
- Rationale is transparent.
- Assumptions are stated.
- Next steps are undefined, not implied.

The goal is to invite ownership, not to manufacture agreement.

The next stage— Affirmation—will further narrow the funnel, calling the body to respond faithfully to what has been discerned together.

Questions to Ask Before Proceeding

Before moving forward, leaders should pause and ask:
- *Do these recommendations emerge naturally from what we have learned?*
- *Are we naming options honestly, not strategically?*
- *Have we resisted the urge to control the outcome?*
- *Are we prepared to trust the body in the next stage?*

If the answer is yes, the journey may continue.

Recommendation does not decide the future. It clarifies the paths before it. And clarity, held with humility, prepares the way for shared ownership.

Next Chapter: The Affirmation Stage

The next chapter is the **Affirmation Stage.** This stage will unify and propel the group toward implementation. But first, the members will need to shoulder the courage to approve godly, thoughtful recommendations.

CHAPTER SEVEN

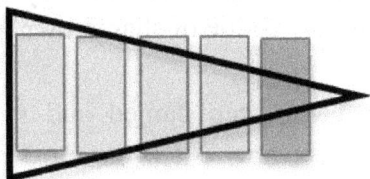

Stage 5

Affirmation

Embracing the Direction Together

"But the wisdom from above is first pure, then peaceable, gentle, open to reason, full of mercy and good fruits, impartial and sincere."—James 3:17

Every movement of renewal eventually arrives at a holy moment—the moment of *YES*. After listening, examining, presenting, and recommending, now comes a time when the body of Christ must decide together: *Will we walk this path God has set before us?*

Welcome to the **Affirmation Stage!** Affirmation transforms recommendations into resolution and plans into partnership.

It's not just a business vote or a formal motion. It's a sacred act of unity when leaders and members together affirm the direction they believe the Holy Spirit has revealed.

Affirmation is the discipline of shared ownership.

After pathways have been named and recommendations clarified, the process now enters its most relational stage. Affirmation is not about securing approval or avoiding resistance. It is about inviting the body—church or association—to respond faithfully to what has been discerned together.

This stage does not ask, *Can we move forward?*
It asks, *Will we move forward **TOGETHER**?*

The Purpose of Affirmation

The purpose of Affirmation is **alignment, not unanimity.**

Healthy affirmation does not require that every person feel equally enthusiastic. It requires that the body understands the recommendations, trusts the process that produced them, and is willing to move forward in unity—even while holding questions or grief.

Affirmation narrows the funnel by transforming clarity into commitment.

Why Affirmation Cannot Be Rushed

Leaders often underestimate the emotional and spiritual weight of this stage. By the time recommendations are presented, some people have only recently begun to grasp the reality leaders have been processing for months.

Affirmation requires time for understanding, prayer, and honest response.

When leaders rush this stage:
- Trust erodes.
- Resistance hardens.
- Decisions feel imposed rather than discerned.

Affirmation protects the integrity of the entire process by honoring the pace of the people.

The Power of Agreement

The Psalmist wrote, *"How good and pleasant it is when brothers live together in unity .... for there the Lord commands the blessing."* (Psalm 133:1,3)

God blesses unity—not uniformity, but the Spirit-born agreement. When the people of God come together around a shared conviction, heaven leans in. The Affirmation Stage isn't just procedural—it's spiritual. It represents a collective response to the voice of God.

In a world where churches often fracture over preferences and personalities, Spirit-led affirmation is a testimony to grace. It tells the world, *"We have listened, we have discerned, and we have chosen to walk together."*

What Affirmation Is—and Is Not

Clarity at this stage depends on restraint.

Affirmation IS:
- An invitation to shared discernment.
- A call to unity and trust.
- A spiritual response, not merely a procedural one.
- A moment of communal responsibility.

Affirmation IS NOT:
- A sales pitch.
- A pressure-filled vote.
- A referendum on leadership.
- A guarantee of enthusiasm.

When affirmation is framed incorrectly, people are asked to choose sides rather than walk together.

Why The Affirmation Stage Matters

The Affirmation Stage matters because it is where vision turns into shared conviction and unity. It is the point at which a group confirms, through prayerful agreement, that their discernment aligns with God's leading. This stage ensures that decisions are not just good ideas, but God's ideas—rooted in spiritual consensus and empowered by collective faith.

Affirmation is essential for three reasons:

1. It creates ownership.

When people affirm a direction together, they no longer see it as the leader's idea—it becomes *our* calling.

2. It establishes accountability.

Unity means shared responsibility. Everyone has a role to play in living out the decision.

3. It invites blessing.

God's power flows most freely where His people walk in agreement. Affirmation aligns the church with the Spirit's movement.

Without affirmation, recommendations remain mere suggestions. With it, they become sacred commitments.

A Biblical Model of Affirmation

In Exodus 24, after Moses read the Book of the Covenant to the people, Scripture says, *"They responded with one voice, 'Everything the Lord has said we will do.'"* (Exodus 24:3)

119

That's affirmation—a unified, collective *"YES"* to God's direction.

Similarly, in Acts 6, when the apostles recommended appointing deacons, the text says, *"This proposal pleased the whole group."* (Acts 6:5)

That phrase—*"pleased the whole group"*—reflects the harmony of hearts that affirmation brings. The Spirit of God had prepared the people so that when the moment came to decide, unity flowed naturally.

The Spiritual Posture of Affirmation

Affirmation is not about winning a vote; it's about discerning a voice—the voice of the Spirit.

The right posture is humility, gratitude, and dependence. Leaders should say: *"We have sought God's direction together, and now we humbly affirm what we believe He has shown us."*

In this stage, prayer is more important than procedure. Before the decision is made, take time to pray corporately, thanking God for clarity and asking Him to seal unity.

When affirmation is done prayerfully, it becomes an act of worship, not just an act of governance.

How to Facilitate the Affirmation Stage

Facilitating the Affirmation Stage requires both spiritual sensitivity and practical guidance. It's helping people move from discussion to decision—creating space for prayer, listening, and unity to emerge. The facilitator's role is not to persuade but to guide the group toward a confident, Spirit-led "YES" that brings peace and shared purpose. The following should serve as a guide to the facilitator's actions:

1. Clarify the process.

Remind people of the journey: *"We began by listening to God (Exploration), faced our reality (Examination), shared our findings (Presentation), and prayerfully discerned next steps (Recommendation). Now we stand together to affirm God's direction."*

2. Restate the vision simply.

Review the key recommendations and explain their purpose clearly and concisely.

3. Provide opportunity for questions.

Allow honest dialogue before any decision is made. Transparency builds trust.

4. Invite prayerful reflection.

Pause for collective prayer before the group votes, responds, or signs a covenant of commitment.

5. Make the moment meaningful.

Consider reading Scripture, singing, or lighting candles as a symbol of unity and light for the journey ahead.

6. Document the affirmation.

Record the decision in official minutes or create a written covenant signed by leaders or members. Tangible expressions of agreement solidify commitment.

The Leader's Role in the Affirmation Stage

During this stage, the leader becomes a *shepherd of unity*. His role is crucial in nurturing both clarity and unity among the people. As a shepherd, he is protecting the spirit of harmony, ensuring that every voice is valued, and keeping the focus on God's direction. Through humility, prayer, and discernment, the leader helps the group affirm God's will with confidence and peace.

Here's how:

- **Model humility.** Express gratitude for everyone's participation and honesty throughout the process.
- **Celebrate the journey.** Remind the group how far they've come and how God guided each step.
- **Emphasize togetherness.** Use "we" language, not "I" language.
- **Keep focus on the mission.** Unity is not the goal itself—it's the foundation for the mission.

When leaders demonstrate humility and gratitude, affirmation feels less like a decision and more like a shared testimony. Affirmation should be invited with humility and clarity.

Leaders should:
- Recount the journey briefly and clearly.
- Name the recommendation honestly.
- Explain the rationale without defensiveness.
- Acknowledge the cost and uncertainty.
- Invite prayerful response.

Language matters. The tone should communicate trust in God's guidance rather than confidence in human planning.

Affirmation as Covenant

In many cases, it helps to express affirmation in a tangible covenant. It can be written on the ballot as a written statement such as:

"Having sought God's direction through prayer, examination, and discernment, we, the members of [Church/Association Name], affirm these recommendations as our next faithful steps. We commit to walk together in unity, accountability, and obedience, trusting God to accomplish His purposes through us."

Share that a *"YES"* vote is an act of shared agreement. An option is to invite leaders and members to sign this covenant as a symbolic act of shared commitment.

A covenant turns agreements into accountability and vision into a vow.

Navigating Resistance During Affirmation Stage

Even after months of prayer and preparation, not everyone may agree. That's normal. Resistance during the Affirmation Stage is natural, as change often stirs uncertainty or fear. Wise leaders view resistance not as opposition to overcome but as an opportunity to listen, clarify, and build trust. By responding with patience and grace, leaders can turn tension into deeper unity and strengthen the body's confidence in God's leading.

When differences remain, respond with grace:

- **Listen sincerely.** Every concern deserves to be heard.
- **Respond gently.** Avoid defensiveness. Affirm the person, even if you can't affirm their position.
- **Maintain transparency.** Make sure the process and rationale are clear.
- **Keep praying for unity.** True affirmation is not forced—it's formed by the Spirit.

Celebrating Affirmation

Reaching the Affirmation Stage is a milestone worth celebrating—it marks the moment when prayer, discernment, and unity converge. When a church or association reaches this stage, it deserves celebration. This is where God's people joyfully recognize His direction and joyfully walk together in obedience. Celebration affirms God's faithfulness, strengthens shared resolve, and reminds everyone that renewal is both His work and His gift.

The following could serve as important reminders of God's grace and faithfulness:

- Reading Scriptures about unity and mission (John 17, Philippians 2).
- Sharing testimonies of what God has done during the process.
- Publicly stating the affirmed direction.
- Praying for empowerment and blessing.
- Sharing communion as a sign of spiritual unity.

Celebration reinforces identity: *We are one people, called for one purpose.*

The Fruits of the Affirmation Stage

When the Affirmation Stage is done prayerfully and biblically, three outcomes typically follow:

Part II: The Six Stage Process

1. Peace.

The anxiety of uncertainty fades. People sense God's presence and purpose.

2. Participation.

Members move from spectators to stakeholders. Ownership replaces apathy.

3. Power.

The Spirit moves freely in a unified body. Momentum builds naturally for implementation.

The Affirmation Stage is the breath before the next step—the deep inhale before the church (or association) begins walking out what she has agreed to do.

2 Action Steps of the Affirmation Stage

The Affirmation Stage is where the church or association seeks unity before moving forward. Up to this point, the Renewal Team has prayed, examined the facts, listened to leaders, and prayerfully crafted recommendations. In this stage, the focus shifts from presenting information to discerning agreement together. The Affirmation Stage places high value on spiritual unity, not organizational pressure.

This stage includes two crucial steps: the Discussion-Only Meeting and the Vote-Only Meeting. Together, these two steps protect the spirit of renewal by ensuring decisions are made prayerfully, wisely, and with shared conviction before God.

Action Step 1: The Discussion-Only Meeting
The Discussion-Only Meeting provides the church or association with an intentional space to process, question, and understand the recommendations before any decisions are made. This meeting is not about convincing or campaigning, but about clarity, transparency, and trust. Members are free to ask questions, request explanations, and express concerns in a safe environment without the pressure of an immediate vote. This step encourages healthy dialogue, respectful listening, and shared discernment. When handled with grace and patience, the Discussion-Only Meeting becomes a vital opportunity for the body to move toward unity, allowing hearts to align before the people seek God's will through a vote.

Action Step 2: The Vote-Only Meeting
The Vote-Only is a sacred moment when the church (or association) responds to God's leading with a clear decision. Since discussion has already taken place in the previous step, this gathering focuses solely on prayer and the vote itself. There is no debate, no convincing, and no prolonged conversation at this meeting—only a unified posture of seeking God's will together. The purpose is to allow the church or association to affirm (or not affirm) the recommendations with peace and confidence. When done

prayerfully and respectfully, the Vote-Only Meeting strengthens trust, honors unity, and marks a defining step forward on the journey of renewal.

A Leader's Prayer

Lord, thank You for leading us this far in unity and grace.
As we stand together to affirm Your direction, seal our hearts in peace.
Protect us from pride, fear, and division.
Let our agreement bring joy to heaven and witness to the world.
May this moment of affirmation mark a new beginning—not just of plans, but of partnership in Your mission.
Bind us together, Lord, in love and purpose, so that all we do may bring glory to Your name.

Reflection Questions

1. What signs of unity have you seen emerging through your process so far?

2. How can you make the Affirmation Stage more meaningful than just a procedural vote?

3. What practical ways can you express and celebrate unity in your context?

4. How will you continue to guard unity after affirmation and into implementation?

Closing Thought

Affirmation is more than a decision—it's a declaration. It's the body of Christ standing together to say, *"We've heard God's voice, and we will follow."*
> When unity replaces uncertainty, momentum begins to build.
> When hearts align around the same mission, energy is released.
> When affirmation becomes action, the church starts breathing again.

This is the sound of renewal—the collection *"YES"* of God's people echoing through heaven and earth.

The Renewal Process using the Funnel Graph has narrowed. Focus is clear. The future is calling.

Now, it's time to move forward from process to plan—to ask and trust the Lord to breathe life into the plan.

Knowing When to Move Forward

Affirmation has done its work when:
- People understand the direction.
- Leaders sense growing alignment.

- Conversations shift toward *how*, not *whether*.
- Trust remains intact, even amid grief.

At this point, the funnel narrows one final time.

Questions to Ask Before Proceeding

Before proceeding, leaders should pause and ask:
- *Do people trust the process that brought us here?*
- *Have we invited response without coercion?*
- *Are we prepared to shepherd those who remain unsure?*
- *Do we sense permission to move forward together?*

If the answer is yes, the journey may continue.

Affirmation does not remove uncertainty. It confirms commitment. And commitment, rooted in trust, prepares the way for faithful action.

Next Chapter: The Implementation Stage

The next chapter is the **Implementation Stage**. It shifts the focus from decision to action. This is where strategic steps are taken, systems are strengthened, and the work of renewal begins to take shape in daily ministry. Implementation is when faith becomes practice, and where the future God intends begins to unfold.

CHAPTER EIGHT

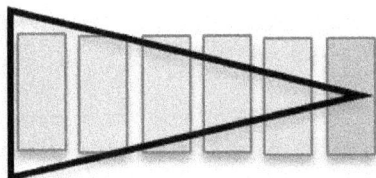

Stage 6

Implementation
Walking It Out

"But be doers of the word, and not hearers only, deceiving yourselves."—James 1:22

There comes a moment in every renewal journey when the time for prayer, planning, and preparation gives way to **movement.**

Welcome to the **Implementation Stage**—the place where clarity meets courage, where the Spirit-breathed plan begins to take shape in real time.

The Implementation Stage is not the end of the Renewal Process—it's the beginning of a new life cycle. Everything that has been discerned, examined, presented, recommended, and affirmed now comes alive through obedience.

The Renewal Process using the Funnel Graph has narrowed to its final stage, and what flows out of it is not just a plan, but a renewed people on mission.

Implementation is the discipline of faithful obedience.

After months of listening, examining, presenting, discerning, and affirming, leaders may feel both relief and resolve. A direction has been clarified. A commitment has been made. The temptation now is to move quickly—to demonstrate progress, regain momentum, and justify the process. Implementation resists that temptation.

This stage does not ask, *How fast can we move?*
It asks, *How faithful can we walk?*

The Purpose of Implementation

The purpose of Implementation is **obedient follow-through**. Implementation is not about proving the process worked. It is about stewarding what has been discerned with care. Faithful implementation reflects humility, patience, and attentiveness to the Spirit's ongoing guidance.

This stage completes the funnel—not by closing it tightly, but by grounding action in shared commitment.

Implementation Flows from Affirmation

Implementation does not begin with planning. It begins with alignment. Before any steps are taken, leaders should confirm:

- Affirmation was clear and genuine.
- Roles and responsibilities are understood.
- Communication remains transparent.
- Trust has been preserved.

When implementation is disconnected from affirmation, action feels imposed rather than owned. When it flows from affirmation, movement feels purposeful—even when difficult.

What Faithful Implementation Looks Like

Faithful implementation is marked by several characteristics.

1. Clarity over Complexity
Plans should be clear, simple, and realistic. Overly complex strategies often signal anxiety rather than wisdom.

2. Phased Movement
Implementation unfolds in stages. Early steps focus on alignment and learning rather than immediate results.

3. Ongoing Discernment
Implementation remains attentive. Leaders continue to listen, pray, and adjust as needed.

4. Pastoral Care
Change always involves loss. Leaders must shepherd people through grief as well as hope.

5. Patience with Fruit
Faithfulness is measured in obedience, not immediacy.

Guardrails for Healthy Implementation

The Renewal Process includes guardrails designed to protect implementation from common failures.

- **Do not overpromise.** Be honest about timelines and challenges.
- **Do not oversell success.** Avoid celebratory language that ignores cost.
- **Do isolate leadership.** Continue to communicate openly.
- **Do not confuse activity with progress.** Reflection remains essential.
- **Do not abandon prayer.** Dependance on God must remain visible.

These guardrails help ensure that implementation reflects the spirit of the process, not just its conclusion.

Measuring Faithfulness, Not Just Outcomes

Implementation inevitably invites evaluation. But leaders must be careful about what they measure.

Helpful questions include:
- *Are we acting in alignment with what we discerned?*
- *Are relationships being honored?*
- *Are leaders communicating consistently?*
- *Are we responding to challenges with humility?*

Numerical outcomes may matter, but they are not the primary measure of faithfulness at this stage.

The Spiritual Nature of the Implementation Stage

Many see the Implementation Stage as merely practical: budgets, calendars, committees, and administration. But at its core, the Implementation Stage is deeply spiritual.

In Ezekiel 37, God told the prophet to prophesy to the bones—and as he spoke, the bones came together, flesh formed, and breath entered. The vision didn't come alive until obedience activated it.

Likewise, the Spirit breathes through action. The Implementation Stage is where faith expresses itself through follow-through.

James 1:22 reminds us, *"Do not merely listen to the Word, and so deceive yourselves. Do what it says."*

Renewal is not complete until obedience is visible.

From Paper to Practice

The Implementation Stage turns plans on paper into a transformation in people.

This is the season when strategies become ministries, recommendations become routines, and vision becomes visible. It's where energy, alignment, and accountability begin to converge.

Leaders often describe this stage as both **exhilarating** and **exhausting**—and that's because movement always brings progress and pressure.

The good news is that when the plan has been birthed through prayer and affirmed in unity, the Spirit empowers the work. The goal is not flawless execution but faithful continuation of the renewal God has begun.

A Biblical Model: The Early Church in Acts

In Acts 2, after Jesus' followers had prayed and waited as He instructed, the Holy Spirit came. They didn't stay in the upper room—they stepped into the streets.

Implementation happened immediately:
- They preached the Gospel boldly.
- They baptized new believers.
- They gathered in homes for teaching and fellowship.
- They met needs, shared resources, and multiplied disciples.

That's what Spirit-led implementation looks like—action that flows directly from divine empowerment. It was organized (*they devoted themselves to teaching, fellowship, and prayer*), but it wasn't mechanical. It was structured *and* Spirit-filled—orderly, yet alive.

That's the model for every implementation that follows the Renewal Process: structure and Spirit working together to sustain life.

Why Implementation Often Fails

Many well-intentioned plans never make it past the "affirmed" stage. They die in the notebooks, file cabinets, or meeting minutes. They fail not because they lack vision, but because they lack follow-through. The journey from

Part II: The Six Stage Process

Affirmation to Implementation requires discipline, accountability, and sustained leadership. Without intentional action, even the most prayerful decisions can fade into forgotten documents rather than becoming living realities.

Here's why:
1. **No clear ownership.**
   Everyone agreed with the plan, but no one was assigned responsibility to act on it.

2. **No timeline.**
   Without measurable milestones, even good intentions fade.

3. **No accountability.**
   When progress isn't reviewed, priorities drift.

4. **No prayer.**
   Churches or associations sometimes move from prayerful discernment to practical exhaustion, forgetting that the Spirit who led them still must empower them.

Implementation isn't just about doing more; it's about doing *the right things* with the right heart.

When Implementation Requires Course Correction

Implementation rarely unfolds exactly as planned. New information emerges. Unanticipated resistance arises. Circumstances change.

Course correction is not failure. It is stewardship.

Leaders should remain willing to:
- Revisit assumptions.
- Adjust timelines.
- Clarify communication.
- Re-engage prayer and listening.

The funnel does not disappear at implementation. Its posture remains—a commitment to discernment even in action.

The Long View of Renewal

Implementation is not the end of renewal. It is the beginning of a new season of faithfulness.

Some fruits will be immediate. Others will be slow. Some outcomes will surprise leaders—both with joy and with sorrow. Through it all, faithfulness remains the measure.

Renewal is not sustained by strategy alone. It is sustained by trust, humility, and obedience.

How to Begin the Implementation Stage

Beginning the Implementation Stage is about turning conviction into coordinated action. It requires clear steps, defined responsibilities, and a shared commitment to follow through on what has been affirmed. This stage transforms prayerful discernment into practical obedience, ensuring the vision becomes reality in the life of the church or association. The following steps guide the leader.

1. Revisit the affirmed recommendations.

Review the commitments made in the previous stage and confirm that everyone understands what has been affirmed.

2. Assign ownership.

Every task or initiative should have a responsible person or team. Ownership drives momentum.

3. Set realistic timelines.

Create a clear but flexible schedule. Implementation works best in 90-day action windows—short enough to stay focused, long enough to see progress.

4. Start small, build momentum.

Focus on 2-3 early wins that are visible and achievable.

Success builds confidence.

5. Celebrate progress publicly.
Share stories of what God is doing as the plan unfolds. It keeps energy high and gratitude visible.

6. Pray constantly.
Implementation without prayer is execution without inspiration.

When the plan is bathed in prayer, ownership, and patience, results will come naturally.

The Role of Leadership in Implementation

Implementation requires both **management** and **ministry**. Leaders must move from discerners to developers—from facilitators of conversation to builders of culture.

Here's what it looks like:
- **Stay visible.** Regularly communicate progress and gratitude.
- **Stay adaptable.** Adjust methods without losing mission.
- **Stay spiritual.** Keep prayer and dependence central.
- **Stay humble.** Credit the team, not yourself.
- **Stay hopeful.** Encourage persistence when challenges arise.

Part II: The Six Stage Process

The Implementation Stage is where leadership maturity is most tested and most revealed.

Building Systems for Sustainability

Healthy implementation requires systems that sustain momentum without stifling the Spirit.

Sustainability doesn't happen by accident—it's built through intentional systems that support ongoing health and growth.

Developing clear structures, processes, and rhythms helps ensure that momentum continues long after the initial enthusiasm fades. Strong systems allow the vision to endure, adapt, and bear lasting fruit for God's glory.

The following are the key systems to establish:

1. Communication System:
Keep everyone informed through updates, newsletters, or testimonies.

2. Evaluation System:
Meet quarterly to review progress on each initiative. Ask, *"What's working? What needs adjustment?"*

3. Support System:
Encourage teams and leaders through coaching and prayer partnerships.

4. Celebration System:
Mark milestones—new ministries launched, goals achieved, lives changed.

5. Spiritual Renewal System:
Schedule seasons of rest and reflection to keep the process spiritually alive, not just organizationally busy.

Systems don't replace the Spirit—they protect the space where He works.

Dealing with Discouragement

Every implementation season faces setbacks—plans delayed, volunteers stepping away, results slower than expected. When that happens, remember: delay doesn't mean defeat. Renewal rarely moves in straight lines. Encourage your team to keep perspective:

- Celebrate faithfulness, not just fruit.
- Focus on progress, not perfection.
- Remind each other that obedience is success in God's eyes.

As Galatians 6:9 promises, *"Let us not grow weary in doing good, for at the proper time we will reap a harvest if we do not give up."*

Implementation requires that kind of steady faith.

Keeping the Spiritual Fire Burning

When implementation stretches long, it's easy to shift into autopilot—to manage the plan but forget the Presence. Guard against that by continually returning to worship and prayer. Invite testimonies from those experiencing renewal firsthand. Revisit the early vision that stirred hearts at the beginning of the journey.

Spiritual renewal must remain the center of organizational renewal. Otherwise, the Renewal Process using the Funnel Graph becomes a formula instead of a flow of life.

The Fruits of Implementation

When churches and associations faithfully walk through the full Renewal Process, the Implementation Stage becomes a living testimony to God's power.

The fruits of the Implementation Stage are the visible signs that faith and obedience have taken root. When God's people act on what He has revealed, transformation begins to unfold—in lives, ministries, and communities. These fruits remind us that renewal is not just a plan fulfilled, but a testimony of God's power working through willing hearts.

Common results include:
1. Renewed morale.
People feel hopeful again because they see tangible change.
2. Stronger unity.
Teams that once worked in silos now collaborate in mission.

3. Missional clarity.
Every activity begins to align with purpose.

4. Spiritual vitality.
Worship deepens. Prayer increases. The Spirit's presence becomes palpable.

Implementation is where renewal stops being a plan on paper and becomes a pattern of life.

10 Action Steps of the Implementation Stage

The Implementation Stage is where renewal becomes visible. This is the point where the church or association moves from decisions to action, from planning to practice, and from agreement to obedience. During this stage, the Renewal Team guides the church or association in implementing the affirmed recommendations through a series of intentional and incremental steps. Specific assignments are given, timelines are established, and new ministry systems begin taking shape. Consistent communication remains vital, ensuring the church or association stays informed, unified, and encouraged throughout the process.

Action Step 1: Reaffirm the Mandate and Direction. Before any actions take place, leaders must re-center the church or association on the "why."

- Revisit the affirmed vision, priorities, and recommendations.
- Re-share the spiritual convictions behind the direction.
- Clarify what is changing—and what is not.
- Emphasize unity, trust, and shared responsibility.

Action Step 2: Assign clear leadership ownership. Every recommendation must have a named leader or team.

- Identify a point person or team for each recommendation.
- Define authority, responsibility, and accountability.
- Ensure all understand *what* they are leading and *why*.
- Provide spiritual and relational support for those carrying the load.

Action Step 3: Establish Realistic Timelines and Milestones. Momentum requires structure.

- Break large recommendations into smaller, achievable steps.
- Establish short-term wins (30-60-90 days).
- Set milestones check-ins for progress and adjustment

- Avoid overloading the calendar or the congregation.

Action Step 4: Align Structures, Systems, and Resources.
Vision stalls when systems resist change.
- Review committees, teams, and decision-making processes.
- Align budget priorities with affirmed direction.
- Adjust job descriptions, ministry expectations, or workflows as needed.
- Eliminate or pause ministries that compete with the new direction.

Action Step 5: Communicate Early, Often, and Consistently. Silence breeds anxiety. Clarity builds trust.
- Share progress reports regularly.
- Celebrate steps forward, even small ones.
- Explain delays or adjustments honestly.
- Use multiple channels: worship, newsletters, meetings, digital platforms.

Action Step 6: Provide Training and Equipping. New direction often requires new skills.
- Train leaders and volunteers for new roles and expectations.
- Provide coaching where change feels uncomfortable.
- Reinforce biblical foundations for adaptive leadership.
- Normalize learning curves and growth.

Part II: The Six Stage Process

Action Step 7: Monitor Health, Not Just Activity.
Implementation is about more than completed tasks.
- Watch for spiritual health, morale, and unity.
- Listen carefully for feedback and resistance.
- Address fatigue or conflict early.
- Guard against mission drift.

Action Step 8: Measure What Matters. Use meaningful
indicators rather than raw numbers alone.
- Track alignment with mission and values.
- Observe engagement, ownership, and discipleship
  pathways.
- Monitor ministry effectiveness and impact.
- Adjust metrics as the season unfolds.

Action Step 9: Stay Flexible and Responsive.
Implementation is not a straight line.
- Make course corrections without abandoning vision.
- Distinguish between wisdom and resistance.
- Remain open to the Spirit's redirection.
- Protect unity while allowing adaptation.

Action Step 10: Anchor the Process in Prayer. Renewal is
sustained spiritually, not mechanically.
- Keep prayer central in leadership gatherings.
- Invite the congregation into focused prayer rhythms.
- Pray over decisions, leaders, and transitions.
- Continually surrender outcomes to God.

This stage is not meant to be rushed. Implementation is most effective when progress is steady, prayerful, and measured.

The Renewal Team must continue to depend on the Holy Spirit, remembering that renewal is spiritual work.. One of the greatest dangers of this stage is drifting back into old patterns and assumptions, so discipline, accountability, and regular evaluation are essential.

A Leader's Prayer

Lord, You have spoken, and we have listened.
You have led, and we have followed.
Now, breathe on the work of our hands.
Make every action an act of worship.
Give us endurance when progress is slow, wisdom when
decisions are difficult, and joy when fruit begins to appear.
Keep us humble, Spirit-led, and faithful—until what began
as a vision becomes reality, and Your church stands
renewed for Your glory.

Reflection Questions

1. What specific actions or initiatives need to begin immediately in your Implementation Stage?

2. Who will take responsibility for each one, and what timeline will guide them?

3. How will you celebrate early wins and maintain energy for the long haul?

4. How will you ensure prayer and spiritual vitality remain central throughout implementation?

Closing Thought

When leaders move forward in faith, when teams serve in unity, and when obedience meets opportunity, the Church begins to move with the rhythm of resurrection.

The bones live. The breath flows. The mission continues.

The God who began the work will be faithful to complete it.

Questions to Ask Before Proceeding

As implementation begins, leaders should pause and ask:
- *Are we acting from trust rather than fear?*
- *Are we caring for people as much as plans?*
- *Are we willing to adjust without abandoning direction?*
- *Are we still listening for God's guidance?*

If the answer is yes, the work ahead—though demanding—will be fruitful. Implementation does not complete the story. It carries it forward.

PART III

Shepherding Renewal

(Chapters 9-12)

Part III: Shepherding Renewal

CHAPTER NINE

The Role of the Pastor, AMS, and Key Leaders

"And He gave the apostles, the prophets, the evangelists, the shepherds and teachers, to equip the saints for the work of ministry, for building up the body of Christ."—Ephesians 4:11-12

Renewal is sustained by shared leadership, not heroic leadership. Renewal is never carried by one leader alone.

Yet in nearly every renewal journey, the temptation toward *singular* leadership quietly emerges. People look for a face, a voice, a guide—someone to absorb uncertainty and bear responsibility. Over time, that pressure often settles on one person: the pastor, the AMS, or a particularly gifted leader.

When this happens, renewal becomes fragile.

The Renewal Process is designed not only to guide churches and associations through discernment but also to **protect**

leaders from isolation and unhealthy dependency.
Renewal is sustained not by heroic leadership, but by **shared faithfulness, clear roles,** and **mutual trust.**

This chapter exists to name those roles clearly—and to free leaders to lead well without carrying what was never meant to be theirs alone.

Renewal Reveals Leadership Dynamic

Renewal does not create leadership problems. It reveals them.

As clarity increases, expectations intensify. As direction emerges, scrutiny follows. Leaders who once operated comfortably within familiar systems now find themselves navigating emotion, resistance, grief, and hope simultaneously.

In this environment:
- Strong leaders may over-function.
- Quieter leaders may disengage.
- Informal power structures surface.
- Old assumptions are challenged.

Without clarity of role and posture, even well-intentioned leaders can unintentionally undermine the process.

Renewal requires leaders who understand *what is theirs to carry—and what is not.*

The Pastor's Role
Witness. Anchor. Shepherd.

The Pastor as Witness. In the life of the local church, no role is more visible—or more vulnerable—than that of the pastor. During renewal, pastors often carry layered expectations that few articulate, but many assume.

Pastors are expected to:
- Provide spiritual leadership.
- Maintain unity.
- Communicate clearly.
- Absorb criticism.
- Offer hope without guarantees.

This weight must be honestly owned

The Pastor as Spiritual Anchor. The pastor's first responsibility in renewal is not strategy, but **spiritual anchoring**.

This includes:
- Keeping prayer central in leadership conversations.
- Framing renewal biblically rather than pragmatically.

- Modeling dependence on God rather than confidence in plans.

When pastors anchor renewal spiritually, they remind the church that this is not a project to manage, but a calling to discern.

The Pastor as Shepherd of People, Not Outcomes. Renewal surfaces grief long before it produces clarity. Pastors shepherd people through:
- Fear of loss.
- Anxiety about change.
- Anger rooted in misunderstanding.
- Grief tied to identity and memory.

Much of this shepherding happens quietly—through hallway conversations, phone calls, hospital visits, and late-night prayers.

This work is invisible, but essential.

The AMS / Associational Leader's Role

The Association Mission Strategist (AMS) and other associational leaders occupy a unique space in renewal— close enough to care deeply, but distant enough to see clearly. Their authority is not positional. It is relational.

The AMS as Guardian of the Process. AMSs protect the Renewal Process by:

- Holding leaders to posture rather than pace.
- Asking questions that slow urgency.
- Naming patterns without assigning blame.
- Refusing to shortcut discernment.

Often, the most faithful contribution an AMS can make is not offering answers, but **creating space for clarity to emerge**.

The AMS as Interpreter of Context. Because AMSs walk alongside multiple churches, they carry perspective that local leaders may not see:

- Cultural and demographic shifts.
- Patterns across congregations.
- Broader kingdom movements.

This perspective should never be wielded as leverage. It is offered humbly, as a gift to discernment.

The Disciple of Neutrality. AMSs must guard neutrality carefully. When associational leaders:

- Advocate too strongly for outcomes…
- Align with factions…
- Rush clarity for the sake of momentum…

Trust erodes quickly.

AMSs serve best when they protect discernment, not direction.

The Role of Key Lay Leaders

Carriers of Trust. Lay leaders often shape renewal outcomes more than pastors or AMSs realize.

They carry history.
They hold relationships.
They influence tone in quiet ways.

Bridges. Lay leaders serve as bridges between leadership teams and the broader body by:
- Transitioning process into everyday language.
- Modeling patience and trust.
- Reinforcing unity in informal spaces.
- Asking honest questions publicly.

When lay leaders trust the process, others follow.

When lay leaders are undervalued. When lay leaders are sidelined:
- Suspicion grows.
- Communication gaps widen.
- Resistance hardens.

Renewal weakens when leadership is perceived as distant or concentrated. Inviting lay leaders meaningfully into discernment strengthens credibility and unity.

Leadership Teams

Shared Discernment. The Renewal Process assumes leadership teams—not individuals—are the primary stewards of discernment.

Healthy leadership teams during renewal:
- Pray together regularly.
- Speak candidly behind closed doors.
- Disagree respectfully.
- Present unified communication publicly.

Unity does not mean unanimity. It means commitment to walk together faithfully.

Guarding Against Over-functioning and Under-functioning. When one leader carries too much, others disengage. When leaders disengage, trust erodes.

Teams must actively resist:
- Allowing the strongest voice to dominate.
- Letting quieter leaders withdraw.
- Assigning emotional labor unevenly.

Part III: Shepherding Renewal

Shared leadership protects everyone.

Navigating Through the Renewal Process

Renewal stretches leaders beyond familiar roles. Pastors feel pulled into administration. AMSs feel pressured to decide. Lay leaders feel caught in the middle.

This tension must be named, not ignored. Helpful practices include:
- Regular role check-ins.
- Clarifying decision authority.
- Reaffirming shared purpose.
- Extending grace when missteps occur.

Role clarity is not static. It must be revisited as renewal unfolds.

When Leaders Disagree. Disagreement among leaders is inevitable—and healthy—when handled well.

Healthy faithful disagreement:
- Happens privately before publicly.
- Seeks discernment, not victory.
- Respects the roles of others.
- Preserves relationships.

Public disagreement among leaders erodes trust quickly. Alignment behind closed doors protects unity in public.

Caring for Leaders Through the Long Journey. Renewal is not only hard on churches. It is hard on leaders. Leaders need:

- Encouragement.
- Rest.
- Prayer.
- Safe spaces to process doubt and fatigue.

Ignoring leader health undermines renewal at its core. Leaders who care for one another model the very health they seek to cultivate.

A Word to Leaders Who Feel the Weight. If renewal feels heavier than expected, that does not mean you are failing. It means you are leading honestly.

You were not called to carry this alone.

You were not called to guarantee outcomes.

You were called to lead faithfully—together.

Final Reflection for Leaders

Pause and ask:

- *Are roles clear and honored among us?*
- *Is leadership shared or concentrated?*
- *Are we modeling humility, patience, and trust?*

Part III: Shepherding Renewal

- *Are we caring for one another as leaders?*

Renewal is sustained not by gifted individuals but by faithful leaders walking side by side.

CHAPTER TEN

The Effective Renewal Leader

"...whoever would be great among you must be your servant, and whoever would be first among you must be your slave, even as the Son of Man came not to be served but to serve, and to give his life as a ransom for many."—Matthew 20:26-28

The Renewal Process is more than a model; it's a journey. And every journey needs a leader.

In every church or association that has walked through the Renewal Process, one truth has proven consistent: the process rises or falls on the presence of wise, patient, Spirit-led leadership. That Renewal Leader may be a pastor, a mission strategist, a consultant, a denominational resource person, or a lay facilitator—but regardless of title, the role is the same: **to help God's people to discover a future that is thriving and bringing Him great glory!**

Part III: Shepherding Renewal

This is the role of the renewal leader—no matter the title.

The Heart of the Renewal Leader

The Renewal Leader's primary goal is not to impress people with expertise, but to invite them into a journey to discover a future that is thriving and bringing God great glory!

He helps the group keep moving forward through each stage without skipping or stalling. He protects the pace, maintains focus, and creates space for the Holy Spirit to work.

To lead this way requires a particular kind of heart—one that is:
- **Patient** enough to wait for God's timing,
- **Present** enough to listen well,
- **Prayerful** enough to discern what words to speak,
- And **humble** enough to stay in the background when others need to shine.

Renewal leading is not about taking control of the process. It's about releasing control to the Holy Spirit while guiding people safely through the journey.

The Renewal Leader as a Shepherd

A Renewal Leader is more than a facilitator of meetings—he is a shepherd of moments. He walks beside people as truth surfaces, conflict emerges, and hope takes root. He senses when to challenge and when to comfort, when to push for clarity and when to pause for prayer.

In many ways, the Renewal Leader mirrors Jesus' pattern with His disciples—asking questions, guiding reflection, and letting learners arrive at their own revelation.

Jesus didn't hand out step-by-step manuals. He walked with people. He listened, asked, modeled, and released. That's what healthy renewal leadership looks like in the Renewal Process.

Renewal leaders embody grace and truth simultaneously—speaking truth gently and guiding with conviction.

What a Renewal Leader Does (and Doesn't) Do

A Renewal Leader plays a vital part in guiding a team or teams through the renewal process, but that role has clear boundaries.

He doesn't make decisions or dictate direction—instead, he asks questions, offers perspectives, and helps others discover what God is already revealing. His purpose is to empower, not control, fostering ownership and spiritual growth within the group.

A Renewal Leader does:
- Ask good questions that uncover assumptions.
- Listen actively, without rushing to fix.
- Keep the group focused on the purpose of each stage.
- Encourage prayer and reflection before each action.
- Provide accountability for next steps.
- Model humility, hope, and faith.

A Renewal Leader does not:
- Make decisions for the group.
- Push their own preferences or agenda.
- Move faster than people can follow.
- Use authority to force outcomes.

The Renewal Leader's power lies not in control, but in *influence*—the quiet authority of presence and wisdom.

A Biblical Picture of the Renewal Leader

In Acts 18, we find a powerful image of leading in the relationship between **Aquila, Priscilla, and Apollos.** Apollos was eloquent, gifted, and passionate—but his understanding was incomplete. Scripture says Aquila and Priscilla *"took him aside and explained the way of God more accurately."*

Notice their posture: they didn't humiliate or control him; they guided him privately, humbly, and helpfully.

That's renewal leading—coming alongside others to refine, strengthen, and encourage them. The best Renewal Leaders do not stand in the spotlight; they steady it so others can stand there with confidence.

The Skills of an Effective Renewal Leader

An effective Renewal Leader combines spiritual discernment with practical leadership skills to help others move forward with clarity and confidence. He listens deeply, asks insightful questions, and helps others see both possibilities and obstacles. At the heart of these skills is a commitment to serve rather than steer—guiding others to discover God's direction for themselves. The following is a list of practical skills:

1. **Listening**—Hearing not just words, but the heart. Great leaders discern what's beneath the surface of what's being said.

2. **Questioning**—Asking open, honest questions that provoke reflection.
  "What makes you say that?"
  "How do you sense God leading in this?"
  "What would faithfulness look like right now?"

3. **Clarifying**—Helping people find language for what they're feeling or sensing.

4. **Encouraging**—Calling out progress and celebrating faithfulness.

5. **Focusing**—Keeping discussions aligned with purpose, not drifting into unrelated debates.

6. **Reflecting**—Helping groups learn from their experiences rather than simply moving on to the next task.

These are not business skills—they are *pastoral disciplines* that flow from a heart rooted in Scripture and love.

The Posture of a Renewal Leader

The posture of the Renewal Leader is one of humility, patience, and attentiveness to the Holy Spirit. Rather than driving outcomes, the renewal leader creates space for God's people to listen, discern, and respond together. Their quiet strength lies in guiding the process—not controlling it—so that unity and clarity can emerge naturally. The renewal leader's posture is vital—and requires humility and a prayerful presence.

While the Renewal Leader is a steady companion, he is also the guide for specific gatherings or discussions.

A good Renewal Leader knows how to:
- Create a safe environment for honesty.
- Balance participation so every voice is heard.

- Manage time without rushing the Spirit.
- Summarize and synthesize what's said.
- Always point the conversation back to the central question: *"What is God saying to us in this?"*

The Renewal Leader sees the *whole journey* yet serves the *moment at hand*.

Guiding Without Controlling

One of the most challenging lessons for a Renewal Leader to learn is to relinquish control. There's a temptation to "push" people through the Renewal Process—to accelerate progress, tidy up emotions, or preempt conflict. But growth takes time, and forcing it always backfires.

Real change occurs when people take ownership of the journey. The leader's task is not to pull them along but to walk beside them, asking questions and providing clarity when needed.

Think of Jesus again: He didn't drag His disciples to maturity. He invited them into discovery. Renewal leading is about invitation, not imposition.

Common Challenges Renewal Leaders Face

Renewal Leaders often encounter challenges that test their

patience, discernment, and perseverance. From resistance to change to unclear expectations or stalled momentum, these moments can feel discouraging. Yet, each challenge is an opportunity to depend more deeply on God's wisdom through the very tensions that shape lasting transformation.

The following are some of the challenges:

1. **Impatience.**
   The process may move more slowly than you'd like. Trust God's pace.

2. **Emotional fatigue.**
   Listening deeply takes energy. Remember to rest and recharge spiritually.

3. **Resistance from others.**
   Some leaders will push back against the process. Don't take it personally. Let the Spirit work.

4. **Role confusion.**
   Leaders aren't fixers or bosses. Stay in the lane of guidance and support.

5. **Fear of failure.**
   Not every process produces quick success. Faithfulness is your measure, not outcomes.

Building a Renewal Leadership Culture

Healthy renewal multiplies when renewal leadership becomes a culture rather than a position. That means Renewal Leaders within churches and associations begin to lead one another by asking better questions, listening more deeply, and encouraging growth rather than enforcing control.

Imagine an association where pastors gather not to compare numbers, but to encourage one another in the renewal of prayer, perspective, and perseverance. Imagine churches where leadership meetings are more like discernment sessions than board debates.

That's the kind of transformation that outlives the process.

The Renewal Leader and the Holy Spirit

Ultimately, every leader of renewal is a co-laborer with the Holy Spirit.

The Spirit is the true Guide, the unseen Leader behind every human leader. He provides wisdom beyond knowledge, discernment beyond data, and power beyond personality. That's why prayer must remain the Renewal Leader's greatest tool.
When unsure what to say, pray.
When the room feels tense, pray.

When progress stalls, pray.
When hearts begin to soften, thank Him and pray again.

The best renewal leading happens when the Renewal Leader's voice becomes background music and the Holy Spirit's voice takes center stage.

Asking Hard Questions

Renewal does not begin with action. It begins with permission. Permission to slow down. Permission to listen. Permission to ask questions without rushing toward answers.

Not every church or association is ready for renewal—not because God is unwilling, but because leaders are often unprepared to face what renewal reveals. Readiness is not about desperation or decline. It is about posture. It is about whether leaders are willing to tell the truth together and remain united regardless of where that truth leads.

This chapter is *not* an invitation to start the process yet. It is an invitation to discern readiness.

Readiness Is a Posture, Not a Crisis

Many churches enter renewal conversations only after reaching a breaking point. Attendance has plateaued. Giving has declined. Conflict has surfaced. Energy has faded. While a crisis can create openness, it is not a requirement for renewal.

Some of the most faithful renewal journeys begin in seasons of apparent stability, when leaders sense misalignment before decline becomes visible. Others begin when the pain can no longer be ignored. In either case, readiness is not defined by circumstances but by posture.

A ready church is not one that has all the answers. It is one willing to ask honest questions—and wait for honest responses.

The Questions That Signal Readiness

Churches ready for renewal tend to ask different kinds of questions. They move beyond tactical concern and into deeper discernment.

Instead of asking, *How do we fix attendance?* They ask, *What is God forming—or reforming—among us?*

Instead of asking, *What programs should we add?* They ask, *What assumptions are shaping our decisions?*

Instead of asking, *How do we get people back?* They ask, *Who are we called to reach now?*

These questions require humility. They slow conversations. They resist easy answers. And they often surface tension among leaders who see the future differently.

Readiness means leaders stay at the table when tension emerges.

Signs a Church May Be Ready

While no checklist can guarantee readiness, certain indicators consistently appear in churches and associations prepared to engage in a renewal process.

A willingness to listen. Leaders invite voices beyond the usual circle. They listen without defensiveness and resist the urge to explain or justify.

A shared concern for faithfulness. Conversations shift from protecting structures to stewarding mission.

Patience with process. Leaders understand that discernment takes time and are willing to wait together.

Commitment to unity. Even when opinions differ, leaders prioritize relationships over outcomes.

Openness to change—or release. Leaders acknowledge that not everything currently in place must be preserved.

None of these qualities is dramatic. But together, they create an environment where renewal can be approached with integrity.

Warning Signs of Premature Engagement

Just as important as recognizing readiness is identifying when a church or association should not move forward yet.

Some common warning signs include:
- Leaders are already committed to a specific outcome.
- Renewal language is being used to justify predetermined change.
- There is little trust among key leaders.
- Listening feels threatening rather than formative.
- The process is being rushed to relieve anxiety or pressure.

Entering renewal without readiness often increases resistance rather than clarity. It can deepen division, erode trust, and harden positions. Slowing down this part of the process is not failure—it is wisdom.

Why Some May Resist the Renewal Process

Most people want results—and that's not wrong. But in our

urgency to see fruit, we may skip the stages that make fruit sustainable. We want the harvest without the planting, the celebration without the cultivation.

Here are three common reasons people may resist process:

1. **Impatience.**

We want quick outcomes. The modern world runs on instant everything—instant food, instant communication, instant gratification. But God's kingdom moves at the speed of transformation, not technology.

2. **Pressure.**

Leaders may feel the expectation of people who want fast change or visible growth. In that pressure, we sometimes sacrifice discernment for speed. We act before listening.

3. **Pride.**

Deep down, we like to be the hero who solves problems immediately. Process requires humility—it reminds us that we are participants in God's work, not the producers of it.

Process-thinking invites us to slow down, not because we're lazy, but because we're faithful. The Renewal Process reminds us that every stage matters and that skipping stages leads to shallow change.

The Role of Leadership at the Threshold

Pastors, AMSs, and key leaders play a critical role at this point. Their task is not to push the process forward, but to protect it.

Protection looks like:

- Refusing to oversimplify complex realities.
- Naming fears without amplifying them.
- Holding space for prayer and reflection.
- Modeling humility and patience.

Leadership at this stage is quiet. It resists urgency. It creates room for shared discernment rather than unilateral direction.

This is often where leaders feel most exposed. To proceed requires courage—not to lead loudly, but to lead carefully.

Deciding to Proceed with the Renewal Process

Before engaging any formal stage of the Renewal Process, leaders should ask a simple but weighty question together:

Are we willing to tell the truth—and stay together—no matter where it leads?

If the answer is yes, even tentatively, the journey may continue. If the answer is no, then honesty itself is a faithful place to pause.

There is no shame in waiting. Renewal is not earned through effort. It unfolds in God's time, through God's people, with God's wisdom.

Preparing to Enter the Renewal Process

If readiness is emerging, the next step is not action but orientation. Leaders must understand the nature of the process they are about to engage—its rhythm, its guardrails, and its purpose.

The chapter that follows will introduce the framework that shapes the journey ahead. It will explain why the process narrows before it clarifies, and why discernment precedes decision.

For now, the invitation remains the same:
Slow down.
Listen well.
Stay together.

The process will come soon enough.

A Leader's Prayer

Holy Spirit, make me a faithful guide in the journey of renewal.
Teach me to listen more than I speak, to ask more than I answer, to wait more than I rush.

Help me discern what You are doing and join You there.
Guard my heart from pride, weariness, or control.
Let my presence bring peace, not pressure; clarity, not
confusion; encouragement, not exhaustion.
May I be a coach that points people to You, until the
churches I serve no longer depend on me, but walk in the
confidence of Your voice alone.

Reflection Questions

1. In what ways can you grow as a listener?

2. How might you cultivate a coaching culture among the leaders you serve?

3. Which stage of the Renewal Process tends to challenge your patience the most as a leader?

4. How can you depend more deeply on the Holy Spirit when leading others through the Renewal Process?

Closing Thought

The renewal leader plays one of the most crucial roles in the Renewal Process—not as a commander, but as a companion.

His job is not to steer the ship, but to help the crew hear the captain's voice.

Part III: Shepherding Renewal

When Renewal Leaders lead with humility, patience, and prayer, they create a safe space for renewal to take root. They should model what Spirit-led leadership looks like—steady, gentle, courageous, and full of grace.

In the end, the greatest success of a Renewal Leader is not that people followed *them*, but that people learned to follow *God* together.

CHAPTER ELEVEN

Leading Through Resistance and Grief

"We are afflicted in every way, but not crushed; perplexed, but not driven to despair; persecuted, but not forsaken; struck down, but not destroyed."—2 Corinthians 4:8-9

Resistance is not the enemy of renewal. Unacknowledged grief is.

When renewal work is done honestly, resistance will surface. Leaders should not be surprised by it, nor should they interpret it as failure. Resistance is often the language people use when they are grieving change they did not choose or fully anticipate.

Behind resistance are stories—memories of baptisms, funerals, friendships, sacrifices, and seasons of faithfulness. Renewal threatens none of these, but it often reorders them. That reordering can feel like loss.

Faithful leaders learn to listen beneath resistance rather than confront it head-on.

Understanding the Nature of Resistance

Resistance during renewal usually emerges in subtle ways before it becomes visible. Attendance at meetings may decline. Conversations become guarded. Questions repeat themselves. Tone changes.

Rarely does resistance begin as rebellion. More often, it begins as fear:

- Fear of losing identity.
- Fear of disappointing previous generations.
- Fear of becoming irrelevant.
- Fear of the unknown.

When leaders interpret resistance as defiance, they escalate conflict unnecessarily. When they interpret it as grief, they create space for healing.

Grief as a Leadership Reality

Renewal requires leaders to acknowledge an uncomfortable truth: some things that were good may still need to end. Programs, roles, traditions, or even seasons of ministry can be faithful and finished at the same time.

Grief must be named before it can be processed. Leaders who rush past grief in the name of progress often carry it forward as bitterness or sabotage.

Healthy leadership responses include:
- Naming loss publicly and pastorally.
- Allowing lament without demanding resolution.
- Honoring the past without being governed by it.

Grief does not need to be resolved quickly. It needs to be respected.

Holding Steady Under Pressure

Leaders often feel pressure to "do something" when resistance appears. This pressure can lead to overcorrection—tightening control, escalating authority, or accelerating timelines.

Leading through resistance requires emotional maturity:
- Not taking criticism personally.
- Remaining consistent in posture.
- Holding boundaries without harshness.
- Trusting the process rather than reacting to noise.

This steadiness communicates safety even when people disagree.

When Resistance Persists

Some resistance softens over time. Some do not. Leaders must discern when patience is forming trust and when delay is preventing obedience.

This discernment requires prayer, counsel, and courage. Unity does not mean unanimity. Faithfulness sometimes requires moving forward even when some remain uncomfortable.

Reflection for Leaders

Ask together:
- *What loss might people be grieving?*
- *Have we acknowledged it honestly?*
- *Are we responding with patience or defensiveness?*

Renewal does not eliminate resistance. It teaches leaders how to shepherd through it.

CHAPTER TWELVE

The River of Renewal

"...everything will live where the river goes."—Ezekiel 47:9*b*

Every process has a starting point and an ending point. The Renewal Process, as illustrated using the Funnel Graph, begins with openness and ends with action—with implementation, unity, and momentum.

But what happens when the plan is completed, the goals achieved, and the reports written?

If the Renewal Process was ONLY a process, the story would end there. But it isn't. The Renewal Process is not a one-time project—it's a pattern of life. It's not to conclude with a final meeting, but to continue as a way of thinking, listening, and leading.

When the Renewal Process as illustrated using the Funnel Graph ends, the **flow** begins.

From Structure to Spirit

The Renewal Process, as illustrated using the Funnel Graph featured on the front cover of this book, provides a **structure** for discernment and direction—a guided path through listening, examination, planning, and action. But renewal doesn't come from structure alone. It comes from the Spirit.

When churches and associations complete the Renewal Process, they often ask, *"What's next?"* The answer is simple, but profound: *Keep flowing with what God started.*

You don't leave the **Renewal** behind; you let it become a rhythm of life.
  Exploration becomes a way of *praying.*
  Examination becomes a way of seeing.
  Presentation becomes a way of *communicating.*
  Recommendation becomes a way of *leading.*
  Affirmation becomes a way of *uniting.*
  Implementation becomes a way of *living.*

The structure teaches us *how to flow*, but the Holy Spirit keeps us *flowing.*

A Biblical Picture: The River of Renewal

Ezekiel 47 describes a river flowing from the temple—water that starts small and grows deeper as it moves outward, bringing life wherever it goes. Trees bloom, fish multiply, and deserts turn green. That river is a picture of what happens when the Spirit flows through a renewed people.

The Renewal Process prepares the channel, but the river itself is the work of God. **Once the process is complete, the goal is to stay in the current**.

Renewal is not meant to be bottled; it's meant to be released. When the flow begins, churches (associations) stop asking, *"What's next?"* and start asking, *"Who's next?"*—who can reach, disciple, and equip?

Avoiding the "Completion Trap"

One of the greatest dangers after finishing a renewal process is treating it like a **project accomplished** rather than a **journey continuing**.

Leaders may think, *We did the Renewal Process. We're finished.* But that mindset turns renewal into routine and movement into maintenance. The goal is not to complete the stages **of** the Renewal Process—it's to *become* the stages **in** the Renewal Process.

Healthy leaders of renewal use the same questions, the same spiritual disciplines, and the same posture in every season that follows:
   • When new challenges arise, they **explore** again.

- When growth creates complexity, they **examine** again.
- When God reveal direction, they **present** again.
- When decisions are needed, they **recommend** again.
- When unity must be renewed, they **affirm** again.
- When new plans are launched, they **implement** again.

The Renewal Process is not something you finish—it's something you learn to live in.

Turning Process into Culture

The most successful churches and associations are those that turn process into *culture*. Doing so is where transformation truly takes root. It's the difference between completing a checklist and cultivating a way of life. When renewal is a part of its identity, lasting impact flourishes. Here's how:

1. They normalize prayerful discernment.

Decision-making always begins with listening to God, not human opinion.

2. They value evaluation.

Honest reflection becomes a rhythm, not a rare event.

3. They communicate openly.

Transparency and testimony replace secrecy and speculation.

4. They celebrate collaboration.

Unity and shared ownership become part of the DNA.

5. They stay missionally focused.

Every ministry, meeting, and resource filters through the question: *"Does this help us make disciples?"*

Culture keeps renewal alive long after the process is done.

A Story: Flowing Instead of Finishing

An association completed its Renewal Process journey and was celebrating a successful implementation. Churches had grown more connected, new ministries had launched, and relationships had healed.

At their celebration banquet, the moderator said, *"It feels strange to be done."*

The association's director smiled and replied, *"We're not done. We're just in a new flow."*

He explained how the team planned to keep the rhythm going—quarterly "Exploration Meetings" to pray and listen for God's next direction, annual "Examination Reviews" to assess health, and ongoing storytelling to inspire others.

Later, they were still moving forward—not because of a new process, but because renewal had become their culture.

As one pastor said, *"The Renewal Process taught us how to breathe—now we don't have to think it. We just do it."*

The Renewal Leader's Role in Sustaining Flow

Once the process transitions to flow, the renewal leader's role changes from **director** to **developer**.

The question shifts from *"What do we need to accomplish?"* to *"How can I keep the Holy Spirit's flow unhindered?"*

The following four ways renewal leaders sustain flow:

1. **Model Ongoing Dependence.**
   Keep prayer, humility, and discernment visible in your leadership.

2. **Guard the Atmosphere.**
   Protect unity and keep the organization centered on mission.

3. **Keep Raising New Renewal Leaders.**
   Multiplication sustains movement. Equip others to lead through the Renewal Process.

4. **Stay Spiritually Attentive.**
   Renewal fades when leaders stop listening. Keep your ear tuned to God's whispers.

Sustaining flow means stewarding what God has started.

Signs That Flow Is Continuing

When the flow becomes a way of life, you'll see signs like these:

- Decisions are made prayerfully.
- People speak with faith.
- Vision emerges naturally.
- Conflict is addressed quickly and redemptively.
- Gratitude is contagious.
- Success is measured by faithfulness and fruitfulness.

How to Keep Flow Fresh

Even Spirit-led movements can grow stale if leaders don't continually refresh them. The following are rhythms that keep renewal fresh:

1. Stay closely connected to the source—Holy Spirit.
Make regular space for prayer, fasting, and worship. Without the Source, the river will run dry.

2. Keep telling the stories of God's work of renewal.
Celebrate how God is moving.

3. Revisit the renewal stages annually.
Once a year, walk through a "mini-renewal process" to assess where the Spirit is leading next.

4. Invite new voices.

Renewal grows stronger when fresh perspectives and younger leaders join the flow.

5. **Stay surrendered.**

Hold plans loosely. Be ready for God to redirect at any moment.

As long as humility and dependence remain, renewal will not fade—it will flourish.

A Word About Letting Go

There's a subtle but vital truth about the flow: to sustain it, you must be willing to release it.

The process belongs to God.

The results belong to Him.

The future belongs to Him.

The moment we start clinging too tightly—to methods, memories, or even the stages in the process itself—we risk turning what was meant to flow into something frozen.

Like the Israelites gathering manna, yesterday's grace can't sustain tomorrow's journey. Fresh dependence is required daily.

As leaders of renewal, we must hold every success with open hands and pray, *"Lord, keep the river flowing."*

A Leader's Prayer

Lord, thank You for bringing us through a process of renewal—for guiding us, correcting us, and breathing life into us.
Now teach us how to live in the flow.
Keep us from turning Your movement into a monument.
Help us to walk daily in listening, humility, and obedience.
When we're tempted to stop, stir us again.
When the current feels strong, keep us steady.
And when new directions arise, help us say yes once more.
May the river of Your Spirit never stop flowing through us—until every dry place is watered, and every heart is made new.

Reflection Questions

1. How can your church or association transition from completing the Renewal Process to continuing the flow?

2. Which stages of the Renewal Process should become recurring rhythms in your ongoing ministry life?

3. What practices can you put in place to ensure dependence on the Holy Spirit remains central?

4. How will you measure success differently now that renewal is an ongoing culture rather than a temporary project?

Closing Thought

The Renewal Process was never about charts and stages—it was always about **breath** (life). Life that will bring Him great glory!

The Renewal Process gives structure to what the Holy Spirit is already doing. But once the structure has served its purpose, the Holy Spirit invites us to step into the river—to live in continual renewal.

When the funnel ends, the flow begins. And, in that flow, churches and associations don't just survive change—they become **channels of life** carrying the presence of Christ to the world.

RESOURCE PAGE

FREE
Renewal Resource Kit
(with book purchase)

SCAN QR CODE TO REQUEST

SOME PEOPLE ALSO ORDERED

"BREATH TO THE BONES"
by Johnny Rumbough

"The 'WHY' we need renewal' book

Scan this QR Code to order "Breath to the Bones" - $9.99

End Notes

1. *Pew Research Religious Landscape Study (February 26, 2025): Decline of Christianity in the U.S. Has Slowed, May Have Leveled Off*– by Gregory A. Smith, Allan Cooperman, Becka A. Alper, Besheer Mohamed, Chip Rotolo, Patricia Tevington, Justin Nortey, Asta Kallo, Jeff Diamant, and Dalia Fahmy.

2. *Gallup: 12 Ways to Keep Yours Alive* – by Thom S. Rainer.

3. *Alabama Baptist "The Baptist Paper"(May 17, 2023): Clifton tells church leaders even small churches have large ministry footprint*– by Josh Cook

Acknowledgements

This book was not written in isolation. It was born out of years of walking with pastors, churches, and associations who were seeking God's direction for renewal. To all who opened their doors, shared their stories, and trusted the process—you helped shape what I write about in this book.

I am deeply grateful to the **North American Mission Board of the Southern Baptist Convention**, whose vision, investment, and equipping in church renewal and replanting laid the foundation for my passion to help churches and associations experience a future that brings God great glory. The Replant Lab introduced me to a framework that became both a ministry tool and a personal calling. A special word of thanks to **Mark Clifton**, whose passion for breathing life back into declining churches has inspired so many of us, and to **Dr. Kevin Ezell** for his leadership and encouragement, and for graciously providing the Foreword to this book.

I also express deep appreciation to **James Nugent, Director of Strategies and Revitalization for the South Carolina Baptist Convention**, for his faithful teaching and patient mentoring of me in the renewal process.

Finally, I give all glory to God who continues to breathe life into His Church. May this book be used as a tool in His hands—to revive, restore, and renew congregations and associations for His glory alone.

ABOUT THE AUTHOR

Johnny Rumbough served nearly three decades (1996–2025) as the Associational Mission Strategist of the Lexington Baptist Association in South Carolina. Before that, he was appointed by the North American Mission Board to serve at the Greenville Baptist Association (1991–1996) and was earlier appointed by the North American Mission Board to plant a church in Tega Cay, SC (1985–1990).

He is a graduate of Charleston Southern University (1981) and earned a Master of Divinity from Southwestern Baptist Theological Seminary (1985). In recognition of his leadership and service, Charleston Southern University awarded him an honorary Doctor of Religion degree in 2003.

Across five decades of ministry, Johnny has spoken in hundreds of churches and on numerous platforms. He has served congregations of varying sizes as senior pastor, associate pastor, and interim pastor. He has planted two churches, replanted three, and led dozens through a renewal process. He has trained more than 180 pastor search committees and guided many churches and associations through seasons of renewal. He is the author of *"Breath to the Bones: A Gospel Renaissance of the Local Church."*

Johnny is married to Valerie (English). Together they have two children—Jason (Kelli) and Jamie (Justin)—and six grandchildren: Micah, Luka, Noelle, Liam, Judah, and Charlotte. They make their home in Chapin, South Carolina.

www.ingramcontent.com/pod-product-compliance
Lightning Source LLC
Chambersburg PA
CBHW051827090426
42736CB00011B/1685